Emotional Intelligence
with Eduard

Bucevschi

CONTENTS

1 – FACTS ABOUT EMOTIONAL INTELLIGENCE..................1

Concepts of emotional intelligence 2

Mind and heart – in a symbiotic relationship 3

Diagnostic test and measurement techniques of intelligence quotient ..6

Emotional competences – what you need to learn to become smarter 11

2 – EMOTIONS, BEHAVIORS AND INTERACTIONS 18

The meaning and essence of emotions 19

Brain architecture 23

Interactional theory of emotions...29

3 - YOU AND YOUR EMOTIONS......................................31

Subjective self – are you aware of what you feel? 32

Reflected self – how your emotions are perceived by others 35

The carousel of emotions..36

Rule over your emotions 39

4 – EMOTIONS AND FEELINGS 43

Fear..47

Anger 50

Depression 52

Shame 53

Anxiety 55

Aggression...57

Hate..60

Love 64

Disgust 66

Surprise 68

5 - THE TWO-STEP METHOD OF EMOTIONAL
INTELLIGENCE 70

First Step-Planning 73

Setting the goal 75

Planning and acting 76

Best tactic 78

Action! 80

Notice and name what you feel 80

Discover your emotions 83

Meet your needs 87

6 - EMOTIONAL WORK! 93
DECIDE HOW YOU WANT TO FEEL! 93

Face your emotions: don't deny them! 95

Catching the distance, what does it mean? 96

On the other side of the mirror 99

The case of Guillaume Duchenne 104

Think positive! 105

7 - PRACTICAL EMOTIONAL INTELLIGENCE. IMPORTANT
INFORMATION 108

Time to love yourself...110

Live in harmony with yourself 112

Do not judge 114

8 – YOUR EMOTIONAL INTELLIGENT LOVER 118
Say what you feel 122

Look at the relationship through your lover's eyes 126

Make your partner happy..128

Deepen your bond..132

9 - INTELLIGENT EMOTIONAL PARENT............................136
Listen to what the child says 138

Love your children! 140

Provide support, not criticism...141

Consistency, setting boundaries, predictability 143

Important rules...144

10 - INTELLIGENT EMOTIONAL BOSS 147
Notice, appreciate, give thanks..148

Get to know the team inside out 151

Distance, superiority, emotional coldness, or misunderstood power 153

Be professional!...155

BIBLIOGRAPHY..157

1 – FACTS ABOUT EMOTIONAL INTELLIGENCE

Emotional intelligence – (Emotional Intelligence Quotient, EQ, or Emotional Intelligence, EI) – is the ability to recognize and name emotions properly. It concerns both your own emotions (personal, internal) and other people's emotions (those coming from the outside, non-specific). The ability to emotionally (self-)diagnose is critical in social life because emotions are an integral component of human personality - they are the basis of behavior, actions, and interactions; they decide what we are like and how others perceive us. Emotions, by causing specific reactions to environmental stimuli, affect all living organisms' functioning. This relationship is evident among humans. Taking into account the condition of modern man, it can be safely said that emotions are a powerful force shaping well-being and well-being; understanding them is necessary to find your path to happiness, achieve your goals, achieve personal and professional success, and enjoy the health of your soul and body.[Hashim MJ.]

Emotional intelligence is also a valuable skill in dealing with difficulties and crises, as it is an effective tool in the fight against stress, anxiety, fear, or other destructive feelings. Properly developed EI enables adaptation to external conditions, and facilitates acceptance of oneself and other people, thanks to which a person can acquire wisdom, achieve inner peace, and remain in harmony with the world around him.[Voss RM, M Das J.; O'Connor PJ, Hill A, Kaya M, Martin B.; Salovey, P., & Mayer, J. D.]

Concepts of emotional intelligence

Emotional intelligence first appeared in the early 1990s in the research of two American psychologists - John D. Mayer and Peter Salovey. They created a working definition of EI, viewing it as the totality of intellectual abilities, which - alongside general intelligence (IQ) - is a condition for achieving personal and professional success. EI is acquired during subsequent stages of socialization (so it is the result of social learning processes) and then shaped throughout an individual's adult life. This means that, unlike genetically "programmed" IQ, it can be learned or improved. Mayer and Salovey define EI as "the ability to track other people's feelings and emotions, distinguish them, and use this type of information to guide your thinking and actions". In the course of subsequent in-depth research, psychologists supplemented the concept of emotional intelligence with new aspects. The supplemented definition assumes that EI concerns: adequate perception, assessment, and expression of emotions, access to them, the ability to activate them in situations when they can improve thinking, as well as understanding emotions, applying emotional knowledge, and regulating emotions to enable intellectual development. [O'Connor PJ, Hill A, Kaya M, Martin B.; Salovey, P., & Mayer, J. D.]Emotional intelligence serves the following functions in social life:

› It allows you to control emotions and express them in a manner consistent with the accepted norm;

› enables correct recognition of emotions and their proper interpretation;

› promotes the productive use of emotions and their creative management;

› makes it easier to manage and transpose emotions;

› increases the level of motivation to act;

› makes us liked and respected and trusted;

› improves the quality and influences the number of social contacts;

› expands interaction networks;

› affects self-esteem and well-being;

› makes our lives better and more valuable.

Mind and heart – in a symbiotic relationship

The concept of emotional intelligence proposed by Mayer and Salovey was developed by Daniel Goleman, who presented it more broadly - in connection with other fields of science: biology, neurology, sociology, and anthropology. Thanks to an interdisciplinary view, we have obtained a general picture of the process of IE formation and the conditions influencing its deepening and evolution. The concept of IE has become extremely popular over recent decades - translated into almost all languages of the world and used in various contexts [Bru-Luna LM, Martí-Vilar M, Merino-Soto C, Cervera-Santiago JL.]. Goleman defines EI as a complex of certain abilities - such as perseverance in pursuing a goal despite obstacles or failures, (self-)motivation, controlling impulses, postponing the satisfaction of pleasure, regulating mood, not falling into darkness, not giving in to worries and sadness that limit rational thinking, empathizing with the well-being of others, an optimistic view of what the future will bring. Goleman's theory turned out to be brilliant because it highlighted the fact that a high intelligence quotient (measured on the IQ scale) is not enough to lead a happy and satisfying life, establish healthy interpersonal relationships, find a suitable life partner, make a professional career, gain wealth, power and prestige. , to be admired and respected, to enjoy recognition and respect[Bru-Luna LM, Martí-Vilar M, Merino-Soto C, Cervera-Santiago JL.]. For this, emotional intelligence turns out to be necessary. Many times, people with a high level of IQ (above 150 on the test scale), but with a low IE index, occupy subordinate positions or social positions to people with a lower level of general intelligence, but distinguished by emotional intelligence. Goleman clearly emphasizes that emotionally capable people have an advantage over others in every area of life, from romance and intimate relationships to knowing the unwritten rules in force in the internal politics of various organizations and companies. People with developed emotional skills are usually more satisfied with life and more effective in their actions because they have mastered mental habits that increase their efficiency and effectiveness. People who cannot control their emotions are constantly fighting internal battles that limit their ability to concentrate and think logically, making them unable to focus on their work. People with a low degree of emotional intelligence are constantly rushing somewhere, they have little enthusiasm, so they never complete the assigned tasks. They function chaotically and do not try to put their affairs in order. Everything they attempt fails or leaves much to be desired.[Bru-Luna LM, Martí-Vilar M, Merino-Soto C, Cervera-Santiago JL.]

In many areas of human social functioning (business, trade, politics, education, intimate relationships), what counts is not only the amount of knowledge we have, but also - and perhaps above all - the wisdom of knowing precisely the deepest emotional layers, both our own and other. Only those who understand emotions and interpret them adequately have control over them. Proper management of emotions allows you to achieve joy, harmony, and inner peace and, consequently, build a life model that suits you, act effectively, and remain in harmony with yourself regardless of external circumstances.

The heart (emotions) and the mind (intellect) form a symbiotic relationship. Only when a person takes into account the voice of both in his life does he have a chance to lead a wise and happy life? Neither the heart nor the mind should be "turned off" or drowned out because if we are guided by only one, our judgments and assessment of reality will be deformed and false. The influence of emotions and intellect should be balanced - you need to think logically but also feel intuitively. It is a mistake to interpret events and phenomena only in rational terms and to make only common sense decisions (as in the case of marriages of convenience). However, it is also not good when we are guided only by emotions as in Othello case, thus disregarding the role of reason. Minimizing intellect in everyday life is extremely dangerous because emotional exaltations blind the eyes and weaken vigilance to important facts and events. Only by adopting a dual perspective - intellectual and emotional - allows one to obtain a full overview of the situation.[P. Ekman, 2009, 253]

For many years, in research on human functioning in society, the heart and mind were treated as two extremely divergent categories. The prevailing belief was that an individual's well-being depends primarily on his or her intellectual potential.

The role of emotions was marginalized, seen as the source of human misfortunes - addictions, mental illnesses, phobias, depression, emotional lability, and uncontrollable drives. It was widely recommended to tame emotions because they could lead us astray - they were believed to be a destructive and incapacitating force. Since the Enlightenment, rationalist philosophy has been known, recommending a rational and scientific approach to all social phenomena. If there have been attempts to describe the great power and impact of emotions on human behavior, they were in the context of cynical influence, calculated manipulation, gaining power, or subjugating others. An example of manipulating emotions is brainwashing - a method of taking over another person by changing their thinking using social engineering means of influence (coercion, persuasion, propaganda).

Emotional intelligence is complementary to rational intelligence, which means that it complements a person's general intelligence (often identified with knowledge or education). A person can be considered intelligent if and only if, in addition to a high IQ index, he also has a high IE index. Moreover, emotional intelligence, although it cannot replace substantive knowledge, in some situations turns out to be more important and useful than competencies acquired during many years of education. Therefore, it is worth making an effort to learn this necessary skill in social life.[Salovey, P., & Mayer, J. D., 1990]

The role of general (academic) intelligence is, of course, great and necessary in the social development of an individual, but without emotional intelligence, the knowledge or specialized knowledge often turns out to be useless or insufficient to achieve success. Happiness and fulfillment in personal and professional fields require optimal development of both types of intelligence.

It is worth knowing that neither the emotional nor the rational approach to life is wrong and there is no need to radically change either one. Remember, however, that the approach you present affects your way of thinking, acting, and understanding reality, and therefore - the type of life difficulties and limitations. Generally, every person tends to be on the side of either the heart or the mind, which does not mean that they cannot go a step further and ensure that the influence of both is proportional.

Diagnostic test and measurement techniques of intelligence quotient

It is important to measure your own emotional intelligence before going forward. It will show you the state of your emotions, whether you can correctly identify them, name them, and indicate the source of their origin. The test will also tell you whether your emotions are driving you or whether they are driving you. With this general knowledge, you will make sure you can cope with stress, anxiety, and anxiety; what your relationships are like with other people; Can you talk about feelings, experiences, and internal states? In short - you will find out what level your emotional intelligence is and what areas of this intelligence you should still work on. The test examines various aspects of self-knowledge that make up the overall picture of emotional intelligence. Try to analyze your self-image as honestly as possible and underline the answers that most accurately reflect your beliefs.

I. Appearance:

1. I think I am attractive, although I am aware that not everyone likes me.
2. I don't think I'm attractive and most people think poorly of me or even despise me.
3. Sometimes I have days when I fully accept the way I look.
4. I consider myself an exceptionally attractive person, with no flaws or weaknesses.

II. My self-esteem:

1. I am neither worse nor better than anyone else.
2. I consider myself inferior to others.
3. It all depends on the circumstances - sometimes I think I'm almost perfect, and sometimes I think very badly about myself.
4. I consider myself better than others.

III. What mood or well-being most often accompanies me:

1. My mood tends to stay at the same level: I try to be cheerful and satisfied with life despite the failures or difficulties that occur.

2. I am usually depressed, sad, and negative.

3. I have mood swings: sometimes I'm happy, other times I'm in despair.

3. I am always cheerful and full of spirit, nothing can ruin my mood.

IV. Each new event in my life (change of job, moving, business trip, establishing contacts or acquaintances) causes:
1. I am happy that I will meet new people and places, gain new experiences, and learn additional things.
2. I am very afraid of any changes and I am terrified by the idea that I will have to change my concept of life; I hate risk.
3. If someone takes my place and takes care of all the necessary matters on my behalf, I can accept new things.
4. I get bored easily, so I love new things and change; I am constantly looking for adventures and excesses.

V. I rate my social life as:
1. Successful - I have many friends and close acquaintances with whom I meet often and willingly.
2. Poor- I don't have any close friendships, I rarely go to the cinema, a pub, for lunch or coffee.
3. Moderate – if someone among my friends suggests meeting me, I agree; However, I never initiate meetings myself.
4. Rich - I have a lively social life, I have many casual friends, but none of them is particularly close to me.

VI. If something fails or doesn't go my way:
1. I try to accept failure with equanimity; although I'm sorry, I hope that it will work out in the end.
2. I become convinced that I am hopeless and will never achieve the success I dream of.
3. I give up and stop trying to achieve the goal I initially set.
4. I react very nervously because I hate failure.

VII. If I have to cooperate with people for whom I do not feel sympathy, with whom I cannot find a common language and it is difficult for me to communicate with them, then:

1. I try to keep my emotions in check and remain calm despite conflicts and misunderstandings.
2. I adopt a subservient attitude; For peace of mind, I do everything they tell me.
3. I make no effort to try to communicate with them; I quickly discontinue cooperation, even if we have not finalized the project.
4. I show my dissatisfaction to everyone; I argue and fight for myself.

VIII. I would describe my approach to life and thinking about the present and the future as:
1. Optimistic - I try to think that everything will be fine, although I take into account possible failures.
2. Catastrophic – I torture myself by thinking about the worst things that could happen.
3. Pessimistic – I prefer to think negatively so as not to be disappointed later.
4. Hurrah/enthusiastic – I always look at the world through "rose-colored glasses."

IX. I assess my life so far as:
1. Successful - I wouldn't want to change anything or erase anything.
2. Disastrous – I imagined them completely differently.
3. So-so – I accept them because I know that some people have it worse.
4. Fantastic - that's what I tell myself and others so that they admire me and envy what I have achieved.

X. I assess my time management and fulfillment of assigned duties as:
1. Appropriate - I always do everything on time; I plan the implementation of tasks sufficiently in advance; I try to fulfill the tasks assigned to me on an ongoing basis;
2. Very bad – I never get anything done, I'm always late; I often put things aside and then don't come back to them.
3. I can't plan anything, I'm chaotic and disorganized, but somehow I manage to fulfill my responsibilities.
4. I assign my responsibilities to others; when I feel like it, I do what I have to do; and if I don't have it, I don't perform the tasks assigned to me; I don't care what others think

about it.

I congratulate you for making the effort to complete a diagnostic test that will help you find out your level of emotional intelligence. By reading the generalized description of psychosocial competencies, you will obtain information about the state and level of your emotional intelligence. If you marked most of the answers with "1" - you can consider that your IE is at a good level. You are aware of your flaws, but you also know your strengths. You enjoy life and have the right priorities. You are resistant to failure and can face adversity. Further reading of the book will help you refine and deepen the emotional intelligence that is already within you, and only some dormant layers of it need to be awakened.

If you marked most of the answers "2" - you have a lot of work ahead of you on your emotions, which is worth undertaking to regain emotional balance. You probably feel that your emotions are in a bad state and it causes you great discomfort and maybe even suffering. The basic problem is the lack of control over the destructive moods that overwhelm you due to low self-esteem, a sense of internal shame, and humiliation. Lack of trust in yourself and internal belief in your advantages or strengths leads to a paralyzing fear of being judged by others. That's in turn for others.

If you marked most of the answers as "3", you carry a lot of negative emotions inside you, but with a little effort, you can get rid of them. Your emotional intelligence is not sufficiently developed, but you can nevertheless gain insight into your own emotions and realize which of them limit you and cause failures, conflicts, or stumbles. The first step to emotional health is to know exactly the sources of your emotions - where they come from and their intensity.

If you marked most of your answers as "4", you don't have access to your emotions, and at the same time, you don't understand other people's emotions. A distorted image of yourself and your surroundings makes you unable to realistically interpret both internal and external stimuli. You have disturbed self-esteem - you manifest narcissistic tendencies consisting of exposing and exaggerating the importance of self. Concentrating on yourself causes you to ignore the feelings and needs of those around you, and you consider them to be imaginary or insignificant. You have trouble recognizing other people's efforts, and acknowledging their successes, let alone their victories. The change should be aimed at developing empathy and the ability to understand the emotions of the people around you.

No matter which group you find yourself in, you can try to learn or deepen your emotional intelligence. The condition for success in this field is continuous and conscientious work. Make the first and primary goal of your efforts to reduce negative emotions - those that make everyday functioning difficult for you and the people around you. To achieve this goal, it is necessary to be able to gain insight into your own emotions - to build the most complete information about yourself based on various sources (opinions of other people, subjective thoughts, in-depth observations, objective and parameterized diagnostic tests). A special notebook will help you with this, which will contain a detailed description of your emotional transformation. Call it an "emotion organizer" - this term will suggest the purpose of this notebook. The organizer is used by busy people who have a lot of responsibilities, and such a notebook allows them to organize a lot of activities. The essence of the organizer is the precise division of the day into hours and activities performed. You, too, can use this organizational model when working on emotions. Divide the notebook into individual months and days (plan your transformation process for approximately three months); divide each day into hours. The task involves filling in individual fields regularly and systematically - in the following columns (according to the example below), write down: what happened or what happened to you on a given day at a given time, what you felt then, how you behaved (e.g. "I had a fight", "I cried ", "I burst out laughing") and finally - how others reacted to your emotions ("They felt sorry", "They were offended", "They scolded me", "They praised me", "They expressed admiration", etc.).

Date/time	Event	Emotion	Symptoms of emotion/behavior	How others reacted to my emotions.

Emotional competences – what you need to learn to become smarter

Daniel Goleman indicates that emotional intelligence consists of five main elements: understanding yourself and your own emotions, controlling and managing emotions, self-motivation, empathy, and social relationships. The development of emotional intelligence involves self-improvement in several parallel areas of functioning. No area of psychosocial development can be neglected or omitted because they condition and complement each other.[Mayer, J. D., Caruso, D. R., & Salovey, P., 1999]

Emotional intelligence is a different kind of wisdom. It consists of self-awareness, knowledge of one's feelings and managing them to make healthy life decisions, effective control over emotions such as fear, anger, and depression, as well as the ability to motivate, remain optimistic despite failures, empathy and the ability to empathize into other people's situations and establishing and maintaining good relationships with them.[Christie, A., Jordan, P., Troth, A., & Lawrence, S., 2007; Magnano, Paola, Craparo, Giuseppe, & Paolillo, Anna., 2016]

Emotional intelligence is created by three types of competencies: psychological (concerning the attitude towards oneself), social (concerning relations with the environment), and praxeological (visible in action and readiness to take it). Each of the above-mentioned competencies consists of very important psychosocial skills, including empathy, self-awareness, self-esteem, self-control, cooperation, and adaptive and motivational skills. The detailed composition of psychological, social, and praxeological competencies is presented below.

Emotional intelligence		
Psychological competencies:	Social competencies:	Praxeological competencies:
self-consciousness	empathy	motivation
self-esteem	cooperation	adaptation
self-control	persuasion	conscientiousness
	leadership	

Learning emotional intelligence involves developing and/or improving individual competencies. This task requires a lot of mobilization and effort because each of the three competencies is based on a different set of skills. Therefore, work on emotions should start with good theoretical preparation and acquiring substantive knowledge about what individual competencies are, what abilities they cover, and how the change process should proceed. The first area of competence, i.e. psychological competence, is

› Self-awareness, i.e. knowledge about oneself - one's capabilities, needs, desires, interests, and preferences. In short, everything that makes us happy and sad, what we like, and what makes us uncomfortable. What we do great what we are good at, and what is our Achilles' heel, what fails despite many efforts or requires a lot of effort, while for others it is a piece of cake. Finally, what we want in life (what we strive for, what is important to us) and what we are unable to accept;

› Self-esteem, i.e. a sense of self-worth, potential, possibilities, and strength. Self-esteem should be measurable - neither too high (causes narcissistic behavior) nor too low (causes complexes and prevents full personality development). Adequate self-esteem allows you to recognize your shortcomings and imperfections and highlight your strengths;

› Self-control or self-regulation, i.e. the ability to consciously respond to stimuli from the environment and select them - controlling your emotions, both negative and positive, coping with stress, being consistent with your own beliefs and value system; the ability to defend one's own opinion even at the cost of losing popularity or support, and therefore the ability to set boundaries for myself - what I can and should do, and what is inadvisable or even prohibited for me. It is also the ability to limit yourself or adapt if the situation requires it.

Social competencies include:

› Empathy, i.e. the ability to understand and correctly read other people's emotions, even if they are not expressed directly. Empathy is looking at the world from the point of view of another, identifying with what he feels and how he thinks. It's not about accurately reflecting his feelings, but about becoming aware of them;

› Cooperation and collaboration, i.e. collective participation in performing a task. The condition for their proper conduct is to maintain the emotional identity of the group through declared membership in the team and acceptance of the rules in force;

› Persuasion, i.e. the effectiveness of convincing other people to your arguments by appealing to emotions that will enable and accelerate the undecided to make decisions. Persuasion should be based on agreement and aimed at compromise; it is not about imposing opinions or manipulating, but about presenting reasons reliably and substantively or refuting the partner's thinking patterns;

› Leadership, i.e. the ability to lead a group, the ability to arouse enthusiasm and commitment in people to implement a certain matter. Biographies of great leaders show that they patiently and persistently pursued a vision, drawing multitudes with them. Leadership has a direct relationship with emotions – people only become fully engaged when the issue touches their emotions. A flesh-and-blood leader makes sure that a given undertaking is attractive to the entire group involved in it so that everyone can identify with it and derive material or symbolic benefits from it.

The last area of competence consists of praxeological competencies. They consist of:

› Motivation, i.e. influencing others and yourself to mobilize you to work. Without motivation, your knowledge, skills, and experience have no significance. In practice, motivating means focusing on the effect of your actions and realizing that the effort you make makes sense. Individual steps on the way to the goal must bring joy and satisfaction;

› Adaptation, i.e. the ability to socially accommodate and adapt to changes that are permanently incorporated into life. It does not mean destabilization, on the contrary - it involves strengthening the sense of security despite changing circumstances. The basis of safety is being yourself and being consistent in your values. If you have peace within you, nothing external can disturb it;

› Conscientiousness, i.e. careful and dutiful performance of assigned tasks based on applicable standards. At the same time, you get satisfaction from fulfilling your duties, even if they are tedious and time-consuming. This satisfaction is itself a reward and self-reinforcement.

Try it on yourself

Take into account individual competencies and think about their components. Create your hierarchy of competencies - on a scale of 1-10, rate which competencies you have at a high level and which ones you still need to work on. Perhaps you notice that you do not have some competencies at all and that you should learn them. Knowing your strengths and weaknesses is an important step in working on emotional intelligence. For the task, use the form below, which helps you to work on your emotions.

Emotional Intelligence		
Psychological competencies	Social competencies	Praxeological competencies
On a scale of 1-10 I rate...	On a scale of 1-10 I rate...	On a scale of 1-10 I rate...

Calculate which competencies have the lowest scores. If you rate your psychological competencies as the lowest, you are certainly struggling with the problem of negative thoughts about yourself, lack of knowledge and belief about your strengths - and therefore low self-esteem, fear, and shyness. However, if the lowest rated area is social competencies, you have difficulty establishing and maintaining relationships, persuading others, inspiring others to take action, managing a group, and being a leader. If you rated your praxeological competencies the lowest, start with self-motivation training, which will teach you reliability in performing your duties, conscientiousness in carrying out assigned tasks, and adapting to changing conditions and circumstances.

Put it into practice

Plan the next 14 days in terms of wake-up time, work duration, and how you spend your free time. Separate duties from pleasure and give them precise time limits, e.g. I get up at 6.30, take a shower and eat breakfast, from 7.00 a.m. to 12.00 p.m. Work on a project, 12.30 p.m. - Eat lunch, 1 p.m. - 3 p.m. - Complete your tasks, etc. Of course, the division into times and responsibilities may be different (depending on your mode of functioning and the type of work you do), but you must practice carrying out planned activities as fully and accurately as possible despite unfavorable external circumstances, laziness, the possibility of skipping or postponing a given task. You will certainly find it difficult to follow your plan, knowing that you don't have to. However, thanks to this task, you will learn that organizing some seemingly small and trivial matters will help you organize the big thing that is your life.

Depending on which activities you rated the lowest (i.e. those that cause you the most difficulty), these are the activities you should focus your efforts on working on yourself. The work should be done in small steps, which means that you should select only one element and make efforts to change it.

If social skills are problematic for you, plan to be a stranger for the next month; whether you have an official relationship or are you very close; whether you like and respect them or the opposite). The intensity of contacts and the resulting conversations, arrangements, compromises, and perhaps even quarrels and disputes are an ideal field for practicing the above-mentioned competencies. During meetings, try to activate your emotional intelligence: listen to what others say to you, even if it seems to you that you are wasting valuable time on idle chatter. Imagine that their thoughts, problems, and observations concern you, that you are part of them (to achieve this effect, say: "I imagine what you feel", "I think I know what you are talking about"). Think back to a time when you were in a similar situation and empathically put yourself in the other person's shoes. This will help you look at him in a different, less superficial way. Try to see something valuable in everyone you encounter, even if it is incredibly difficult. Name it and say out loud to the interlocutor: "What I like about you is that...", "I admire you for...", "Your..." is worth praising. After saying one of the suggested formulas, you will immediately notice feedback - the interlocutor will become open, which will make further contact much easier and more fruitful. However, a flattering opinion must be sincere - you must not lie, give false compliments, or pretend to be delighted. Once you have established proper contact with your conversation partner (i.e. you feel comfortable in his company), start achieving the goal of your meeting - establishing cooperation, negotiating the terms of the contract, discussing the marketing strategy, organizing a collection for those in need, organizing an integration trip or a school trip. Listen to everything the interlocutor has to say, then present your opinion. If your opinions differ dramatically, ask your interlocutor what is wrong with your vision and action plan. Carefully consider the answer he gives you. Think about whether you can rationally refute his arguments - if not, think about whether the interlocutor is wrong. Never end a conversation in a categorical way - one that radically cuts off further negotiations. Metaphorically speaking, don't write anyone or anything off, which means not adopting the attitude of, "If it doesn't go my way, we have nothing to talk about." Even if you feel that this is all you want to do at the moment, hold back, hold back, and say: "I'll think about it", "I'll sleep on your proposal", or "I'll think about it." Once you calm down, you will immediately notice that the matter is different than it initially seemed.

Psychological competencies primarily concern the ego - that is, you, not so much in social relationships, but in relationships with yourself. It's all about gaining as much and as accurate knowledge about yourself as possible. On the surface, it may seem to you that you know yourself inside and out, that you know everything about yourself, that nothing can surprise you. Meanwhile, people know little about themselves, sometimes they do not know themselves at all - their possibilities, potentials, and abilities. They cannot realize who they are, what they strive for, and what they want from life and other people. If knowledge about oneself is so poor and limited, how can one talk about in-depth knowledge about others? Remember: only when you get to know yourself, do you have a chance to get to know others. Gaining true knowledge about ourselves is a difficult task because we tend to pretend to be someone we are not. It often happens that we play to ourselves because we think that others will think that we are the mask we are trying to show them. Meanwhile, the lack of honesty with ourselves has disastrous consequences - we will never feel in harmony with ourselves, we will be artificial to those around us. Camouflage, and therefore an image inconsistent with the true character, will be deciphered sooner or later, the game of appearances never lasts forever. The reasons for playing this game are various - either you don't feel accepted, so you want to pose as someone else, or you are self-interested and know that a different image will benefit you. Regardless of your internal motivation, try to be yourself for at least a moment for this exercise. Stand in the truth, accepting that you are as you are - with all your wealth, advantages and disadvantages, weaknesses and strengths, values, and what is poor, fragile, and hopeless in you.[Elizabeth D. Hutchison, 2008, 65]

Be your own judge!

Below is a table divided into three parts. In the first column, write what you are like or how you rate yourself based on your knowledge and beliefs about yourself. In the second column, write down why you think you are, and what evidence supports your thesis, e.g. "I am shy or a failure." The third column should be an assessment of the quality and strength of the evidence collected. In other words, the point is for you to feel like a judge in your case and objectively determine which evidence is strong and convincing, and which is easy to undermine because it is unjustified or unconfirmed.

I believe I am…	Proofs that I am…	As a judge, I assess the evidence as…
1. 2. 3. …		

By doing the above exercise, you may have quickly realized that some of your opinions and judgments about yourself are unfounded - there is no convincing evidence for them. If there is no evidence, then - just like in court - the case has no point and the trial ends. So try to treat the flaws or weaknesses you see in yourself in this way. In a situation where you lack hard evidence or iron witnesses, do not torment yourself, do not accuse, do not punish. Settle it amicably – come to a settlement with yourself, and drop the case.

2 – EMOTIONS, BEHAVIORS AND INTERACTIONS

Emotions have accompanied man since the beginning of his existence. Indirect evidence of evolution indicates that hominids (representatives of the human family) experienced and expressed both positive and negative emotions. Evolutionary adaptive mechanisms are still visible in humans. Just after birth, a baby reacts emotionally (cries, whimpers) when it feels discomfort caused by pain or hunger. When he is given bitter food, he can show disgust, disgust, and revulsion using facial expressions. Smiling can be seen in a three-week-old baby. After two months, emotions of anger, dissatisfaction, and sadness appear in response to the toy being taken away. Fear appears around the seventh month of life; while shyness and embarrassment are observable in a one-year-old child. Over the years, children learn not only to express emotions but also to properly read them on other people's faces.

An international team of five psychologists (Izard, Haynes, Fantauzzo, Slomine, Castle) conducted an experiment that illustrated that even several-month-old children can recognize emotions. In the experiment, mothers were asked to simulate (through facial expressions, gestures, and tone of voice) extreme emotions when playing with their children - joy/satisfaction and sadness/anger. Research showed that babies' faces accurately reflected their mothers' emotions.[Ackerman et al., 1998, 87; Izard and Malatesta, 1987;]

Emotions arose the moment life emerged on earth. They are not only a human feature, but also an animal feature - scientists have long proven that animals also react emotionally - e.g. dogs feel longing for their owners. Elephants experience the death of their offspring extremely intensely, mourning them for a long time. Some animals may show emotions related to motherhood or attachment to a partner. All animals, regardless of species, know what fear is. When faced with danger, they all have a similar physiological reaction - increased heart rate and a periodic increase in body temperature. On this basis, it can be concluded that some emotions are biologically conditioned, an innate property, triggered by external circumstances or environmental changes. Charles Darwin, based on cross-cultural analyses, noticed that some emotions are recognized and understood identically by most people - regardless of their race, origin, place of residence, or gender. It is therefore possible to say with high probability that joy, sadness, surprise, disgust, and anger are innate and instinctive.

John Tooby and Leda Cosmides point out that emotions have developed through evolution to facilitate the body's adaptation to the environment. By performing adaptive functions, emotions enabled survival - in response to a threat, they encouraged people to escape from a predator or compete for access to food. In the course of evolution, subsequent, more complex emotions were created, and the actions that resulted from them. Lorna Marshall states that for centuries emotions have influenced many areas of human social functioning: cooperation, division of labor, collecting food, preparing and sharing food, and raising offspring. Some of these emotions led to competitive behavior and aggression towards strangers, which served to eliminate those who did not belong to the group.[Brase, G.L., 2021]

The meaning and essence of emotions

We all more or less know what emotions are because we experience them every day. Generally, we can say that an emotion is a certain state of mind accompanied by specific feelings and clear reactions. For example, when I feel happy, I smile and am full of enthusiasm, while when I am grieving, I despair, cry, and feel frustrated and discouraged. Etymologically, emotion means being in motion (Latin 'ex movere'), which suggests action, being active, determining, triggering, and reacting. The sources of words highlight the original meaning of emotions - they mobilize us to be active and move us, thanks to them we are not passive, insensitive, and static. Emotions are the source of energy and vitality. They stimulate action, giving life a certain dynamic.

Scientific definitions of emotions are constantly growing. It is difficult to say unambiguously which definition is complete and most precise. Therefore, Nico Frijda distinguishes the following classifications:

1. An emotion is the result of a conscious or unconscious assessment of some event that affects the goals and/or interests of the entity. If the event coincides with the intended goal, the emotion is positive; if not – the emotion is negative.

2. An emotion causes a specific action.

3. An emotion is experienced as some kind of mental state. The effects of emotions are somatic changes, facial and pantomimic expressions, as well as behavioral reactions.[Izard CE., 2009] Emotions cause specific effects on the body's behavior and physiological reactions. This is because "an emotion is a feeling, a reaction arising in response to specific internal or external stimuli, manifested both in the form of an experience and at the physiological and behavioral level."[Fredrickson BL., 2001]

I recommend that you note the emotions you see in the above pictures. Then we will discuss each emotion. So you understand that basic emotions are relatively easy to notice, distinguish, and name. Slightly more difficulties arise when we talk about secondary emotions, i.e. a whole range of individualized experiences - they manifest themselves in different ways, in different circumstances, and the reason for their occurrence may be various events. Secondary emotions include shame, aggression, hatred, and guilt. Paul Ekman states that they are a "mixture of primary emotions," meaning they arise from a combination of two or more primary emotions. Plutchik, on the other hand, believes that in addition to primary emotions, humans can experience a dozen or so secondary emotions resulting from a combination of other emotions. In this way, many times complex emotions are created, which cause new types of experiences and sensations. Plutchik calls the combination of two basic emotions a dyad.[Ekman, P., 1993, 1994, 2003; R. Plutchik, 1980]

Primary emotions	Secondary emotion
joy + trust	Love
trust + fear	Submission
fear + surprise	Agitation
surprise + sadness	Disappointment
sadness + disgust	Regret
disgust + anger	Envy
anger + anticipation	Aggression
anticipation + joy	Optimism
joy + fear	Guilt
trust + surprise	Curiosity

fear + sadness	Despair
surprise + disgust	Shock
sadness + anger	Suffering
disgust + anticipation	Cynicism
anger + joy	Pride
prediction + trust	Fatalism
joy + surprise	Delight
trust + sadness	Sentimentality
fear + disgust	Shame
surprise + anger	Indignation
sadness + anticipation	Pessimism
disgust + joy	Pathology
anger + trust	Dominance
anticipation + fear	Anxiety

Although emotions, like other bodily functions, have evolved and are constantly changing, their expression is similar in humans and animals. Thanks to this, we have no problem recognizing certain emotions, they are obvious to us. Emotions usually appear spontaneously, but sometimes they are faked or masked. Outstanding actors have mastered the art of playing with emotions to perfection, and poker players can "save face." However, in everyday situations, we are unlikely to be able to consciously control all the facial muscles, so you can tell when emotions are not natural. Our experiences are most often illustrated by the face, but it should be emphasized that it is not only the face that takes part in expressing emotions - the eyes, hands, and legs are also important. In addition, the length of the reaction is important - fake emotions are usually longer than spontaneous ones.

The expression of emotions is also the result of social and cultural interactions. Depending on the country, the expression of emotions is different. In Scandinavian countries, restraint and emotional coldness are accepted, while in the Mediterranean countries, openness, closeness, and breaking down bodily barriers are valued. Ignorance of the cultural code leads to misunderstandings, and surprise, and may even cause serious trouble (in Bulgaria, a nod of the head means refusal, in Australia, the OK gesture is considered offensive, with clear sexual overtones, the Polish gesture of hitting the neck several times with an open hand means an invitation to alcohol party, in Romania hitting the neck several times means 'drunk', while among Indians it means: "I'm about to cut your throat"). Therefore, emotional expression and the accompanying gestures and facial expressions may differ in different cultural circles.

Emotional reactions are also related to the dimensions of closeness and distance. Individualistic culture, emphasizing the needs of the individual, assumes restraint in expressing emotions. However, collectivist culture, where the needs of the community come first, is based on the idea of freedom and self-direction, freedom in expressing emotions, multiplying pleasant impressions, and hedonism dominates.

Brain architecture

Despite the unquestionable acceptance of the scientific thesis that modern man is rational and thinking (homo sapiens), one cannot ignore the huge role of emotions in the life of all living organisms. Emotions are extremely important in animal (and therefore human) life because they serve cognitive purposes, which means that they enable relatively accurate knowledge of the surrounding world and a reliable assessment of socio-cultural reality. This is because they guide our reactions and influence our behavior and way of being. Emotions are the first to suggest what to do when the task ahead of us exceeds the capabilities of reason or escapes rational consideration when we are threatened with danger and there is no time to consider how to avoid it.[Coyne, J. C., & Downey, G., 1991] Sometimes they act on the principle of premonitions - many times in the memories of people who miraculously avoided death (during a plane crash, a car accident, the sinking of a ship), there is a memory of a premonition of some tragedy, a prophetic dream or a strong inner voice that told them not to board or take a different route. Thanks to emotions, we are ready to take a specific action, sometimes contrary to logic and common sense.[Cacioppo, J. T., Hawley, L. C., & Bernston, G. G., 2003] This mechanism is evolutionarily conditioned - Goleman notes that emotions help people cope with life's challenges and difficulties they encounter during everyday functioning. Therefore, they played an important role in the survival of the species, being permanently encoded in the body's nervous system as automatic and internal tendencies.[Goleman, D., 1996]

Evolutionary researchers hypothesize that emotional impulses are a permanent element of the nervous system because the survival of the species and phylogeny depend on them. In the light of evolutionary theories, emotions were essential in the process of selecting a sexual partner and the extension of the species, because they largely influenced the choice of sexual partners and, consequently, shaped the genotype and phenotype of the offspring.

To understand why emotions have a fundamental impact on human life, it is necessary to understand the general structure of the most important organ in the human body - the brain. The architecture of the brain is very complex due to the complexity of this organ.

Broadly speaking, the human brain consists of two hemispheres, the brain stem and the cerebellum. Over billions of years of evolution, it has changed its size (it is three times larger than that of other primates), range, and speed of information processing. By comparing brain models in representatives of individual species (reptiles, birds, mammals), one can easily notice that, apart from the fact that the brain changed its volume and capacity, the number of nerve cells and synaptic connections also gradually increased, which made the organisms more and more intelligent and socially adapted. By acquiring further skills, they became able to perform complex mental operations (counting, designing, translation), associating events, combining facts, planning, and remembering.[Bassett, D. S., & Gazzaniga, M. S., 2011]

The oldest part of the brain found in all organisms equipped with a nervous system is the brain stem, which is responsible for basic life functions such as breathing, metabolism, and muscle contraction. It is therefore a condition for the efficient operation of all internal organs, a driving force behind the complex machinery that is the body. Since the limbic system is the core from which the so-called proper brain, it should be recognized that emotions are the basis of our functioning, because they were the first to control behavior and actions, thus creating the original nature of man. The consequence of this is the unusual ability to "sense upcoming events" - characteristic even of lower animal species (rats perfectly sense an approaching flood and are the first to escape). Similarly with people - many times a person does not have to make an intellectual effort to properly understand a given matter or accurately interpret an event. The emerging intuition informs us about potential danger or, on the contrary, convinces us of the correctness of the decisions we have made. It happens that after some time we remember the emotions that appeared when meeting a person for the first time, establishing a relationship, signing a contract, or inviting a business partner to cooperate with us, and we realize that our intuitive beliefs turned out to be correct.

The outer layer of the trunk is formed by the cerebral cortex, which is responsible for emotional processes, which is why it is colloquially referred to as the emotional mind. Phylogenetically, the primary part is the olfactory brain, which influences smell or olfactory sensations and is also responsible for the sphere of emotions and internal experiences. The limbic (limbic) system - the source of proper emotions - is responsible for the experiences we feel when we are overcome with anger, fall madly in love, are filled with joy, fall into despair, etc. In subsequent stages of development, additional structures emerged from the limbic system responsible for cognitive processes, the ability to learn, remember, and think, which enabled man to control his instincts and primitive impulses, making his life easier and nobler (distinguishable from the life of other animals).

Further evolutionary changes contributed to the creation of a new cerebral cortex, thanks to which humans increased their intellectual capabilities, skillfully interpreting information provided by the senses (sight, hearing, touch, taste, smell). The new cerebral cortex made it possible to understand emotions and associate them with a specific situation or event, e.g. in a moment of danger the appropriate emotion was fear, in a moment of mourning - sadness. The ability to properly perceive and experience emotions has contributed to culturally recognized ways of dealing with them - providing support when needed, uplifting, and encouraging. How a person experiences emotions and deals with them proves his intellectual development and level of civilization.

Thanks to an additional layer of the cerebral cortex directly connected to the limbic system, mammals have developed a maternal instinct and a deep emotional bond between the mother and her child. This causes her to take care of her offspring, protect them from danger, and provide food. Animals that do not have this extra layer (e.g. reptiles) do not show any parental feelings, abandoning their offspring. Sometimes it happens that after hatching from the eggs, the young have to find shelter themselves so as not to be killed and eaten by their mother or father.

In a moment of emotional exaltation, the nervous system is stimulated, with particular emphasis on the limbic brain. In this state, it is difficult to control the emotions that drive us - a person stops thinking rationally, analyzing logically, and sensibly interpreting the situation in which he finds himself. In this state, we become angry or furious, unable to control the words we say and the movements we make. The peak of this state is affect - an emotional exaltation during which the individual acts unconsciously, and irrationally, often against his or her own will.

Affect is a state so deep and pervasive that it can lead a person to the most unpredictable acts, e.g. crimes.[Hart, S. D., Hare, R. D., & Harpur, T. J., 1992; Muris, P., Merckelbach, H., Otgaar, H., & Meijer, E., 2017]

Although the example described above is quite extreme and it is rather rare to completely lose control of our emotions, it is important to recognize that we all act under their influence to a greater or lesser extent. The degree of emotional arousal directly translates into the body's physiological responses. When we feel angry, we react aggressively and angrily, become defensive, make a threatening face, and have a sharp look. On the other hand, when we are overwhelmed by happiness, we emanate joy, a sincere smile appears on our faces, and our movements become free and light. Depending on one's well-being, the attitude towards people is also different, as is a higher level of acceptance and tolerance towards people or facts that are different (or contradictory) to the vision of the world in which we stubbornly believe. Emotionally well-balanced people have a positive attitude toward themselves and everyone else, and they accept with great openness and trust what was previously alien or unfamiliar to them. On the other hand, emotionally disturbed people see enemies lurking everywhere, ambushes have been laid, they are constantly on the lookout for tricks, they do not tolerate other people's mistakes or mistakes, and they accuse and blame others for their failures.

We become emotional because of the activity of the amygdala. These are structures (a human has two such bodies, one on both sides of the head) located above the brain stem, resembling an almond. The fundamental role of the amygdala in experiencing emotions was discovered by Joseph LeDoux, an American neurologist. He stated, based on experimental studies on rats, that the amygdala receives impulses flowing directly from the sense organs before they are registered and recognized by the cerebral cortex, which means that some reactions and emotional memories can be shaped without any participation of consciousness and reason.[LeDoux, J. E., 1992;Johnson, L. R., & LeDoux, J. E., 2010]

The amygdala (next to the hippocampus responsible for memory) is an element of the olfactory brain and is responsible for the sphere of emotions - it informs us about what we feel and how we should react. To be more specific: it initiates the production cycle of hormones prompting flight or fight, stimulates the circulatory and muscular systems, and releases additional energy and strength. Norepinephrine is released into the blood, which increases the activity of all areas of the brain, putting it on alert. The senses become more sensitive, characteristic facial expressions and gestures appear, the heart beats faster, blood pressure increases and breathing slows down. The more the amygdala is stimulated, the stronger and longer the emotions experienced become remembered. By depriving a person of the amygdala, we deprive him of the ability to feel and experience emotions. This condition is called "emotional blindness" in the professional literature and is characterized by the absence or weakening of emotional reactions and indifference to situations that commonly cause extreme emotions. It is the amygdala that causes tears to come to our eyes and we start crying in situations of grief, sadness, or bitterness.[LeDoux J., 2012]

Some people, even though they have a properly functioning amygdala, do not understand emotions, and cannot name them or express them (when trying to describe their emotional state, they use an extremely poor emotional vocabulary). They are alexithymics. Even if they feel physiological arousal related to the appearance of some emotion, they do not connect these two facts, e.g. they perceive facial redness as a sign of high temperature in the room, not as a signal of emerging stage fright.

Alexithymia is the inability to identify and express experienced emotions. The disorder was first diagnosed in 1973 by Greek psychiatrist Peter Sifneos. Its causes include stress, constant physical and mental tension, excess work, and lack of relaxation and rest.

Interactional theory of emotions

In the late 1970s, sociological theories began to move towards explaining the role that emotions play in interpersonal and social relationships. Efforts, actions, and decision-making processes, with particular emphasis on the ways of expressing emotions in some cultures.

Arlie Russell Hochschild, an American sociologist, described emotions as the organized actions of individuals that are determined by situational norms and a broader cultural context. It is culture and the patterns it creates that determine what emotions can be shown in specific situations. Hochschild introduces the concept of a "culture of emotions", which - created based on collective imaginations - assumes how and what people should feel in certain circumstances during specific events (e.g. during a funeral one should feel sadness, mourning, depression; and during a celebration Joy and joy are recommended for weddings - both among the newlyweds and guests). Emotional patterns determined by culture are regularly repeated by members of a given community and, consequently, experienced as natural and the only possible ones. Every culture contains the so-called emotional ideologies that determine what attitudes and feelings are adequate, and how one should react to be accepted by the environment. The manifestation and symbol of these ideologies are "emotional markers", i.e. certain events in people's lives that confirm the existence of emotional cultural rules (holidays, traumatic events, ceremonies, rituals).[Hess, U., Beaupre, M., and Cheung, N., 2002]

Regardless of the situation, in the context of emotions, sociologists point to two types of norms: rules for feeling and rules for expressing emotions. The former determines what emotions are appropriate in a given situation, how many there should be, how long they should last, and what direction they should take (positive/negative). However, the rules for expressing emotions indicate the intensity, nature, and style of expressive behavior. It is clear that emotionality, which includes the way of feeling and expressing emotions, influences a person's functioning in society -

his/her behavior, actions, interactions, and the social relations he or she creates.

It often happens in social life that a person cannot reveal his or her true emotions because it would be inadvisable or even dangerous. The individual is forced to adapt to the circumstances, adopt the applicable and desired style of functioning, and control feelings and the way they are expressed. The situation he is in imposes a model of behavior and reaction that prohibits the free disclosure or demonstration of emotions, encouraging them to mask or deny them. This emotional coercion causes great discomfort and stress, as it requires constant control of the Self.

If we are forced to block or suppress emotions, neutralize them, or immediately change negative feelings into positive ones, this difficult emotional work will most probably cause symptoms of depression or a nervous breakdown. Therefore, you should avoid situations in which emotions cannot be vented, cannot be fully revealed, or where the circumstances themselves require them to be hidden. Operating under emotional pressure is always detrimental to your physical and mental health.

3 - YOU AND YOUR EMOTIONS

Life is rushing, external circumstances are changing, new people appear around us, some things lose importance, and we start treating others as a priority. Each change is accompanied by emotions felt more or less intensely. Emotions are always with us - from the most joyful moments, such as falling in love, a wedding, or the birth of a child, to the saddest ones: mourning, divorce, and job loss. Some emotions haunt us and become a nuisance; we miss others because they are rarely ours. We can resurrect certain emotions within ourselves by designing the situation so that they appear. We feel others without our own will when they torment us beyond our control. We want to love and we hate; we want to laugh, but we are constantly depressed and sad.

Life is rushing, external circumstances are changing, new people appear around us, some things lose importance, and we start treating others as a priority. Each change is accompanied by emotions felt more or less intensely. Emotions are always with us - from the most joyful moments, such as falling in love, a wedding, or the birth of a child, to the saddest ones: mourning, divorce, and job loss. Some emotions haunt us and become a nuisance; we miss others because they are rarely ours. We can resurrect certain emotions within ourselves by designing the situation so that they appear. We feel others without our own will when they torment us beyond our control. We want to love and we hate; we want to laugh, but we arc constantly depressed and sad.[Bond, C. F., and DePaulo, B. M., 2006]

Subjective self – are you aware of what you feel?

Awareness of one's own emotions, i.e. the ability to identify, name, specify, and indicate the causes of their appearance, is the basis of emotional intelligence. Only when you realize what you feel and why you feel that way can you begin to explore your own beliefs about yourself and the role of the self in society. To develop or expand emotional awareness, complete the following exercise.

Draw a five-level pyramid. At each level of the pyramid, enter the emotions you would like to work on because they make it difficult for you to function daily (they tire you, they take away your optimism, passion, and joy in life, and they limit you in some respect). Give them a hierarchy - let the base of the pyramid be the emotions that accompany you most often and at the top place the emotions that you never feel. Use the diagram below to complete the exercise.

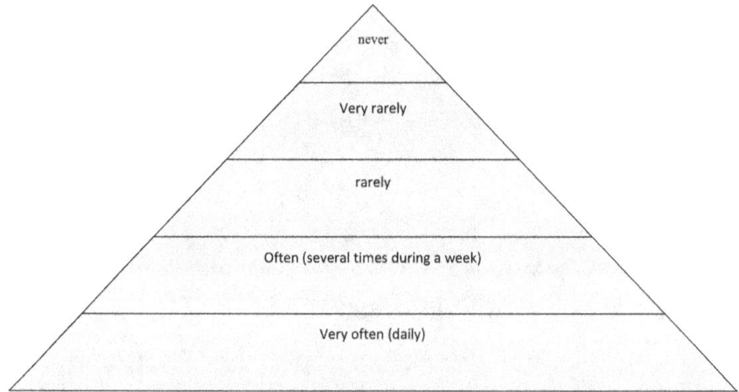

Of all the emotions listed, regardless of the level at which you placed them, circle those that you dislike and do not accept, and consider to be bad and destructive. Use a different color to mark those that are less bothersome but do not bring any benefits and that you would like to get rid of. And now try to examine their nature, to break them down into their parts. To do this successfully, you must have the ability to gain insight into yourself, i.e. the ability to name and analyze what you feel, why you feel that way, how you feel about what you feel, in other words - what emotions give you satisfaction and contentment, and what emotions do not cynical, lazy, rude, full of anger. To gain some initial insight, complete the exercise below.

Be your own judge:
Try to briefly describe your life so far, condensing it into a story of no more than three pages. Recall and describe as precisely as possible the breakthrough events of your life, important dates, meetings, and celebrations. Pay special attention to writing down what emotions you felt at the time. Be honest in your writing - don't embellish anything, don't fantasize, don't think wishfully, and on the other hand, remember not to diminish, doubt, or deny anything. To make writing easier and to ensure the clarity of your argument, follow the points below:

1. Isolate the most important facts from the past (memories of people, events, meetings). Recall as many details as possible about it (what day it was, what the day was like, how it ended).

2. What emotions did you experience then, what mood did you feel, what did you feel and did these feelings seem pleasant or on the contrary, have you ever felt the same or very similar? If so, indicate these situations.

3. How do you evaluate these events from a time and emotional perspective - do they still impress you, move you, or evoke any feelings? Or are you indifferent to them, even though they used to touch you so much?

4. Which parts of the autobiography are the most sad, painful, poignant, and unpleasant for you? Which ones are very joyful, causing a smile and a thrill of positive emotions?

If you have completed the task reliably, you already know a lot about yourself - about your emotions and emotional well-being. You also understand that emerging emotions should not be viewed stereotypically and simplistically which fails to take into account important details about when and why an emotion occurs. You have now gained insight. Insight involves breaking the previously created image of reality by changing perception, which results in a different approach to the matter. Then the problem is looked at more broadly and deeply, gaining a fuller perspective, and allowing for new solutions or innovative ideas. Herbert Simon stated that insight is conditioned by two processes: becoming familiar with the problem and selective forgetting. One gradually gets used to the problem, thinks about it, and analyzes it to see it in a different light, from the other side. If you make a problem less important, it loses its importance - it becomes easier, more bearable, and even trivial. Therefore, it stops tormenting and persecuting you. In turn, selective forgetting, the second process that determines insight, involves erasing some elements of a problem from memory to reduce its scope or strength. When you become familiar with a problem and can selectively forget, it becomes relatively simple, and sometimes you may experience an epiphany that suggests certain solutions.

The basis for change is constant and uninterrupted observation of one's emotions and their assessment in terms of intensity, usefulness, and impact on well-being. The basic goal of insight, apart from the ability to penetrate oneself, is the ability to distinguish permanent and adequate emotional reactions resulting from personality conditions, from transient reactions occurring under the influence of uncontrolled impulses, momentary impressions, or appearing beyond any control. With this knowledge, you will be able to begin the process of self-verification, which, in computer terms, can be described as scanning the emotional program with which you are programmed. The most important thing is that you can face the painful memories, fears, and nightmares that haunt you; so that you can recognize unpleasant emotions, understand them, and control them. Look again at the written autobiography. Mark in color those moments of your life that were unpleasant or sad and evoked similar emotions. Now, having some time and emotional distance from these events, try to recreate individual situations, and make a kind of replay (just like we rewind the recording to hear a given fragment again). Think about how you would behave in this situation now, whether you would react the same way you did then, or maybe you would change your approach 180 degrees. Think about the moment in your imagination and try to participate in it again. Create a new script for your behaviors and reactions. Do the same with moments that fill you with happiness, and give you pleasure and satisfaction. Over time, would you experience them similarly or maybe completely differently? Justify your answer.[Goleman, D., 1996]

Reflected self – how your emotions are perceived by others

Remember that in addition to the subjective self, the self also includes the reflected self. Mead points out that the way you think about yourself depends on the judgments and assessments of people around you. On a conscious and subconscious level, we perceive ourselves as others perceive us. We adopt their attitudes and actions towards each other. At the same time, we evoke in others the thoughts and beliefs that we carry within ourselves[30]. The reflected self consists of the knowledge, hunches, or assumptions a person has about how they are perceived by their surroundings. In the linguistic layer, the reflected self manifests itself in opinions such as: "I think she hates me and doesn't accept me", "I think she is kind and favorable towards me", "I know she loves me because she looks at me with love", "I know he values me because he told me yesterday." There is no doubt that knowledge is closer to objective truth than assumptions and hunches, so treat the facts you know as more important and say more about you. However, opinions resulting from guesses should be rationalized or filtered logically, as they contain numerous falsehoods and cognitive distortions. The way you think that others think and talk about you does not mean that this is the case because people themselves give meaning to their emotions, feelings, and premonitions. So try to verify and constantly control your reflected self, i.e. knowledge about yourself built based on the opinions of others.

Try it on yourself!
List at least 20 positive and negative traits that, in your opinion, best characterize you (e.g. witty, shy, unattractive, composed, gallant, eloquent, etc.). Then ask others (family, friends, acquaintances, neighbors, co-workers) for definitions of individual features (preferably they should write them down on a piece of paper and give it to you). Given these descriptions, consider whether you are a carrier of the trait you attribute to yourself. If, based on this, you decide that a certain characteristic does not correspond to your behavior, stop thinking about yourself in these categories. Constantly monitor your thinking about yourself. Whenever you start to value something in some way, immediately

consider whether this line of thinking is justified and based on facts.

The next step is to gain knowledge about how the emotions you feel and show are perceived by those around you. Emotional deconstruction is important in the sense that based on it you can understand what emotions you have on others, what effects they have on them, how much influence you have on how others feel, and, above all, what they think about you and how they evaluate you. By becoming aware of this relationship, you have a chance to make changes in how you perceive yourself through the eyes of others, and thus solve problems related to self-esteem.

Time to exercise:

Return to the emotion organizer. Draw a three-column table and write down each day what emotion accompanied you the longest today and how others perceived it (what they said, how their behavior changed, how their reactions varied). Once you have completed the table, answer the question of which of the emotions you reveal allow others to think well of you and which make them think less of you.

Day	Emotion	Reaction of others
Monday		
Tuesday		
Wednesday		
Thursday		
Friday		
Saturday		
Sunday		

The carousel of emotions

Psychologists Travis Bradberry and Jean Greaves, examining the nature of emotions, focus on the so-called emotional hijackings – moments when emotions take control of the body. A person reacts suddenly, without thinking, often unreasonably, contrary to logic - thus his actions are devoid of meaning and internal coherence. Many of us have reacted spontaneously and explosively, not following the reaction repertory adopted in a given culture. Usually, however, we realize that our behavior is beyond the norm, and we feel shame, disgust, and embarrassment. Feeling guilty is a sign that the reaction was not adequate to the stimulus that caused it, and the emerging embarrassment is a completely normal and even desirable phenomenon. However, there are also people who, regardless of the situation, always react in extreme ways, contrary to the cultural norm of showing emotions. They are not the masters of emotions, but emotions control them. There are various reasons for this state of affairs, but anyone who succumbs to emotions with impunity and gives in to them always and everywhere has a disturbed emotional structure, will find himself in an emotional trap. To use a figurative comparison, he is like a fly caught in a spider's web, so strong and dense that it forces the insect out of the tangle, deprives it of its freedom, and consequently condemns it to a miserable end.[Luck, T., Luck-Sikorski, C., 2022]

People with emotional disorders often throw things, break things, kick objects, slam doors, publicly humiliate, address those of lower status with superiority, manifest dissatisfaction for unjustified reasons, and deliberately don't pay attention when someone addresses them. These people (with emotional disorders) know what acquaintances to cultivate and what contacts to take care of. To people with real power, they are unimaginably nice and cordial, oozing warmth and kindness. They play both roles with ease and are very comfortable with it.

People with emotional disorders often throw things, break things, kick objects, slam doors, publicly humiliate, address those of lower status with superiority, manifest dissatisfaction for unjustified reasons, and deliberately don't pay attention when someone addresses them. These people (with emotional disorders) know what acquaintances to cultivate and what contacts to take care of. To people with real power, they are unimaginably nice and cordial, oozing warmth and kindness. They play both roles with ease and are very comfortable with it.

Emotional disorders cause significant changes in behavior and endow the personality with certain features, such as manipulativeness, arrogance, the tendency to attack and fight, exploitation, and sabotage. These features create an emotional structure - a kind of skeleton that determines the final shape of how we react and act under the influence of a specific stimulus, in a specific situation. Over time, learned reactions transform into repeated patterns, emotional carbon copies that are resistant to change or rationalization. In a situation of tension, stress, or discomfort, a person activates a reaction model that is known to him from childhood or acquired during socialization and perceived as proven, effective, and beneficial. This mechanism works similarly to comfortable, favorable, and pleasure-giving situations. That's why some people are always happy in the same way, regardless of whether they managed to buy a TV at a promotional price or have had a baby. Still, others cannot express joy at all because they do not know this reaction model at all.[Hart, S. D., Hare, R. D., & Harpur, T. J., 1992]

Depending on the type of emotional disorder, other dysfunctional patterns and reaction patterns are activated. Let's return to the examples of Julia and Wanda described above. Both women have serious emotional disorders, as their dominant emotions are based on the need to humiliate others, and undermine their dignity and value, to raise their self-esteem and improve their well-being. These disorders arose as a result of a combination of genetic predispositions and the acquisition of specific prejudices resulting from experiences, injuries, and the influence of other people. People emotionally unstable are unfulfilled in their personal lives, have bad childhood experiences, and do not accept themselves. They are constantly accompanied by fear, anger, and hostility, which they direct at others to seemingly protect themselves. Their professional position is the only source of any sense of strength and value. Others are either perceived as a source of threat and danger, or they remind us that it is possible to have fulfillment, harmony, and complete satisfaction in life, which emotionally unstable people lack.

The problem of people with emotional disorders is a weak emotional control system and the inability to manage emotions. Remember that emotions should be managed in the same way as a business. If a company is poorly managed and lacks an efficient and effective manager, it will quickly cease operations and go bankrupt. Likewise, if you don't learn emotional management, you will become emotionally bankrupt.

Rule over your emotions

Generally, in social relationships, people tend to match emotions to the context in which they want or are forced to function. They perform "emotional work" - they become emotional chameleons, which means that they choose the appropriate emotional tone to blend in with their surroundings (they feel sad when some unpleasantness or misfortune befalls them; they are happy when they win the lottery). This is a normal and justified mechanism from the point of view of functioning in the group; it is also a necessary, and even advisable, strategy in interpersonal relationships, assuming, of course, that it does not involve any cynical manipulation and calculation. Creating the right emotional image requires considerable skill - just like creating a painting portrait requires a good brush and an artist who knows his craft. People are constantly working on their emotions, adapting to the circumstances - because no one wants to be served by a rude waitress, a stewardess who avoids eye contact, or an arrogant bank clerk.[Ekman, P., 2003]

Work on emotions, including mechanisms of emotion management and preparation of proper self-presentation, takes place at a deep and surface level. It consists of four basic activities:

1. Bodywork – mastering physiological reactions to achieve the desired emotional state (deep breathing to calm down).

2. Surface acting - consisting of the selection of gestures and means of expression by individuals that, in their opinion, will lead to the actual feeling of desired emotions (making gestures of joy at the sight of a colleague to achieve genuine satisfaction with meeting her).

3. Deep action - people try to change their internal feelings, hoping that this will result in the activation of other emotions appropriate to the situation (arousing grief to feel sadness at the funeral).

4. Cognitive work - recalling specific thoughts and concepts related to a given emotion to awaken a feeling appropriate to the circumstances.

Authors like Ekman argue that people often find themselves in situations that require intense emotional labor. Researching TSA personnel scientists found that the responsibility to be pleasant, enthusiastic, and helpful, especially if passengers were rude and arrogant, caused enormous emotional stress. The very fact of constantly controlling emotions and maintaining an image that, no matter what must remain consistent with restrictive rules for expressing and feeling emotions, is extremely exhausting.[Winter J., Currier C., 2015; Denault V., Plusquellec P., Jupe L. M., St-Yves M., Dunbar N. E., Hartwig M., Sporer S. L., Rioux-Turcotte J., Jarry J., Walsh D., Otgaar H., Viziteu A., Talwar V., Keatley D. A., Blandón-Gitlin I., Townson C., Deslauriers-Varin N., Lilienfeld S. O., Patterson M. L., . . . van Koppen P. J., 2020]

Be the judge!

Recall moments in your life when you experienced really strong negative emotions (fear, anger, despair) and positive emotions (joy, fulfillment, satisfaction, happiness). Try to reconstruct these situations as fully as possible - what caused this emotion, when it happened, who was with you then, was a given emotion appropriate in a given situation? When you think about that moment, do you still feel those emotions? Now look at it from the perspective of an outsider who is telling the story but not directly involved. Try to be completely objective and even indifferent to the situation being told. Assess your reactions and behaviors as if they were someone else's (a neighbor, a colleague from work, a friend you meet in a queue for a newspaper, a woman sitting opposite you in a cafe). Looking with a cold, objectified eye, tell how you should react in such situations and what behavior you would recommend to someone. To compare these two types of thinking (your own and other people's), use the example below.

Positive emotions		Negative emotions	
Your perspective	3'rd person's perspective	Your perspective	3'rd person's perspective

By completing the chart above, you are learning an extremely important social skill - dual perspective. This means that you can look at yourself not only through the prism of your personal experiences but also from the position of an objective viewer who looks at you with a cool eye and comments on the visible facts. Even if he includes emotions, they are conditioned by the situational context, not an extremely subjective approach. It's important to always remember that the stick has two ends: what you feel is not necessarily the same as what others feel in a given situation; how you look at a matter does not necessarily correspond to someone else's point of view. Of course, it is reasonable that if something becomes our participation, it engages us more strongly. However, it often happens that we are so egocentric that we do not see the other side, which is very visible to those looking from the outside. And it is this second perspective that facilitates the solution, brings peace, and corresponds to reality. So don't forget that in addition to the obverse, there is a reverse!

Once you develop the habit of assessing events and people using a double lens, you will be able to start working on the next stage of emotion management, which is the ability to control emotions, i.e., take power over them. Emotional control is the ability to deal with impulses that cause specific emotions. A well-functioning control system reduces certain impulses or transforms them into others - those that are better accepted by the environment or more adequate to a given situation (this applies, for example, to crying on the street or in a place full of people, to increased sexual desire when social reasons, it cannot be satisfied, a sudden burst of joy that is not appropriate to express, the desire to throw coffee at a malicious superior or to spank a disobedient child). For most people, this system works quite efficiently (we don't even realize to what extent our reactions are inhibited in certain contexts and circumstances), but some have serious problems with controlling their emotions, which makes social functioning and contacts fundamentally difficult. These people behave completely inappropriately to the situation - their reactions are described by those around them as strange or unpredictable. Living with such people daily is difficult because you don't know who they are and what to expect from them. When we are in their company, we feel uncomfortable and we assume that our safety may be at risk. Therefore, it seems that the basis for proper functioning in a group is controlling emotions, keeping them in check, giving them a specific shape and meaning, adapting to reality, and correcting unusual emotional states.

Lack of emotional control or a dysfunctional control system are the causes of emotional disorders and the inappropriate reactions they cause. If you notice or someone points out to you that your emotions are getting out of control, that you have no influence on them and you are carried away by the wave, make an effort to reorganize your emotional system as soon as possible. If you are a slave of emotions and constantly succumb to passions, you will soon lose yourself in an emotional whirlpool and drown in a flood of moods.

Your emotional detox:
In the process of regaining control over your emotions, you mustn't dwell on any one emotion, do not suppress it within yourself, and do not let it dominate your thinking, perception, or evaluation. Emotions must not be suppressed or denied, you must allow them to flow freely, without paying attention to any of them. This skill is the basis of the Buddhist art of life-based on the principle of harmony of the internal and external worlds. To build such harmony and regain peace of mind, you must cleanse yourself of emotional sediment. Emotions or their remains settle inside you and create a fossilized layer that is difficult to remove.

Sit almost still in a secluded place - turn off the phone, radio, and TV. Make sure that no one and nothing disturbs your half-hour meeting with yourself and emotional detox. Don't think about anything, don't focus on anything or matter, let nothing occupy your attention. Let the emotions flow through your head and don't linger on any of them. Listen to what's happening outside of you - the rain knocking on the gutters, the rustle of trees, birds singing, or - more banally - the sound of a rushing ambulance, the noise of the street, the clatter of a chopstick coming from your neighbor's apartment. Record the sounds you hear, and the images you see, but don't focus on any of them, don't interpret them, don't analyze what's happening. Stay in this state for at least 30 minutes. After doing this emotional detox, you will feel relaxed and cleansed. You will be above what surrounds you or pulls you down.

4 – EMOTIONS AND FEELINGS

People experience different emotions. Some are optimistic, some are neutral, some are pessimistic, and some are painfully realistic. These types of people express and manifest their emotions differently. Depending on which emotions dominate, the behavior and style of functioning in the group are different. Each of us experiences many, sometimes extreme, emotions. We know very well what destructive emotions are (fear, anxiety, anger) as well as building emotions (joy, hope, love). It is not a discovery to say that our emotions directly affect our overall mood and well-being, as well as our physical appearance and health. If we are happy, our mood immediately improves - a smile appears on our face, we are willing to act, we are enthusiastic and optimistic, we exude joy, and those around us perceive us as attractive. However, if we feel sad, our mood immediately begins to decline, which causes an overwhelming sense of emptiness, nihilism, depression, and despair. The face becomes gloomy and gloomy, we adopt a closed attitude that discourages the approach. Remember that emotions decide everything. However, the essence of emotional intelligence is the skillful control of emotions, i.e. regulating the mood, emerging sensations, and mental states through the control of experienced emotions and effects.

If you constantly feel sad, unhappy, and unfulfilled, you struggle with emotional problems, your social relationships are not going well, you are unable to build a lasting relationship, you are not effective in performing tasks, you do not achieve your goals and you feel that no one cares about your likes, does not appreciate and does not respect you, you probably lack emotional intelligence and cannot fully manage your emotions (you let them torment you or impose your style of thinking about yourself and the people around you). Try to change it.

The first stage of change is getting to the heart of emotions, i.e. learning the sources of their emergence, the motives for their appearance, and the reasons why a given emotion can control your behavior. You should be aware of the circumstances in which such emotions appear, with what intensity, and for how long they last. You must know how you start behaving, what actions you take, and what mood you are in then. You must learn to look at your emotions in many dimensions. Only when you see which emotion dominates and what components it consists of can you work through it. Remember that it often happens that under the guise of one emotion, there is another, and what you feel is not what you think it is. Start by screening your emotions, like an X-ray, look at them carefully and see what's inside you.

If you constantly feel sad, unhappy, and unfulfilled, you struggle with emotional problems, your social relationships are not going well, you are unable to build a lasting relationship, you are not effective in performing tasks, you do not achieve your goals and you feel that no one cares about your likes, does not appreciate and does not respect you, you probably lack emotional intelligence and cannot fully manage your emotions (you let them torment you or impose your style of thinking about yourself and the people around you). Try to change it.

The first stage of change is getting to the heart of emotions, i.e. learning the sources of their emergence, the motives for their appearance, and the reasons why a given emotion can control your behavior. You should be aware of the circumstances in which such emotions appear, with what intensity, and for how long they last. You must know how you start behaving, what actions you take, and what mood you are in then. You must learn to look at your emotions in many dimensions. Only when you see which emotion dominates and what components it consists of can you work through it. Remember that it often happens that under the guise of one emotion, there is another, and what you feel is not what you think it is. Start by screening your emotions, like an X-ray, look at them carefully and see what's inside you.

For the next 30 days, carefully observe your emotions. In the organizer, write down every day how you felt, what emotion accompanied you the longest, how you behaved at the time, and what caused such feelings - that is, what was the cause of sadness, happiness, guilt, fear, anger, grief, joy, depression, aggression, shame, etc. At the same time, using a scale of 1-10 (where 1 means the lowest intensity and 10 - the highest), rate the strength of a given emotion. After 20 days of self-diagnosis, take stock. On this basis, you will determine what emotions dominate in your life and what their source is. With this knowledge, begin intensified emotional work.

Of course, the intensity of emotions may vary, but they all come from one emotional stem. To help you identify this stem and thus assign the emotions you feel to the correct group, take a look below.

Emotion intensity	High	Moderate
Happiness	joy, excitement, enthusiasm, energy, delight, favor	contentment, relief, serenity, tenderness, gentleness, favor
Sadness	depression, despair, anguish, suffering, loneliness	depression, breakdown, worry, disappointment, confusion
Anger	rage, anger, agitation, irritation, indignation, disgust	frustration, irritation, disgust, anxiety, nervousness, withdrawal
Fear	horror, panic, trembling, shock	fear, fear, anxiety, uncertainty, fear
Shame	embarrassment,	confusion,

	remorse conscience, feeling of disgrace, humiliation	withdrawal, embarrassment, feeling of low self-esteem

Most failures and life problems result from bad emotions that, unprocessed, projected onto someone, or repressed, profile inappropriate behavior and actions. Bad emotions arise in childhood and have a negative impact on later adult life. The emotional sphere is shaped with the birth of a child and then deepened and modified by representatives of primary groups (parents, grandparents, social circle, neighbors) and secondary groups (teachers, other educational, church, political, hobby, civic institutions, etc.). A lucky person is someone who grew up in a healthy and emotionally stable family. Many, however, do not have the best childhood memories - they experienced emotional abuse, violence, verbal or physical aggression, and no one cared about their safety or provided support. All this causes them to harbor bad, destructive emotions, which over the years become a permanent element of their social personality. Even if we leave the family home and become independent from our parents, we still have an emotional flaw that inhibits or completely prevents the construction of a proper self-image. The consequences of this are significant: we are unable to create a successful partnership, give love, be good and responsible parents, achieve our goals, enjoy trust and respect among colleagues, be appreciated by our spouse or boss, and feel fulfilled and needed.

Many grownups are struggling with stigmas from childhood because of the toxic comparisons with their siblings, neighbors, or classmates. Many parents told their offspring that they were worse, uglier, and stupider than others. Elisabeth, now at the age of 32 still remembers her parents criticizing her appearance, behavior, and way of speaking and behaving. When she got married, she hoped to change all these critiques. Soon she found out that her husband cheated on her because Elisabeth had insufficient commitment, emotional coldness, dryness, insensitivity, and lack of empathy. The second marriage also finished with divorce despite Elisabeth having children with her new husband. She tried to change her behavior and attitude but with no luck. All these only deepened her sense of worthlessness.

This case clearly shows that childhood is the source of many failures and failures in adult life. Even if we have everything - family, education, a strengthened professional position - the wounded and hurt child that is still inside us does not allow us to enjoy it. We constantly replay unpleasant childhood memories, which Sigmund Freud called the "repetition compulsion." Even though we realize that some emotions are destructive and debilitating, we still strive to repeat them, because only then do we feel familiar and safe, and we hope that repeating certain patterns will help us deal with them. This is the road to nowhere. Working through emotions can be compared to the process of cleaning wounds. As you probably know, you should treat the wound gently: first, examine it, then clean it, and finally apply the plaster. If you don't follow the order and tape the wound before cleaning, you risk getting gangrene.

The initial stage, i.e. a detailed look at the emotions, involves becoming aware of what each emotion results from. Remember that they have different etiologies and you are very often unaware of their primary sources. In the following subsections, you will learn about the origins of the most popular and frequently occurring emotions.

Fear

I guess everyone knows what fear is. Everyone can recall moments when they were afraid or even felt panicky, scared, and terrified. Fear is undoubtedly a very unpleasant, blood-curdling feeling, but paradoxically it is an emotion needed in everyday life. It informs us about an approaching threat and encourages us to run away, retreat, in short - to save our lives. This mechanism, justified by evolution, allows us to intuitively sense that the situation we are in is not safe and comfortable.

As an emotion fear is an unpleasant, visceral feeling of anxiety, apprehension, or dread. In most cases, fear is shown in the facial area in crying, increased eye-blink rate, wide open flashbulb eyes, lip retraction, staring eyes with enlarged pupils, tense mouth and even yawning. Fear is also expressed by the body in an exaggerated angular distance, release of apocrine odor, increased breathing rate, mandibular trembling, freeze reaction, bristling hair, increased heart rate, squirm cues, sweaty palms, throat clear and audible tense tone of voice. Fear, apart from informing us about danger and motivating us to escape, also has a second, dark face. It is a bad, paralyzing, destructive emotion that does not allow us to spread our wings or show others the abilities and resources that lie dormant in us. Most people with severe emotional disturbances recall their childhood memories of fear of a parent, teacher, priest, or other person in authority. Fear also appeared in more prosaic situations: before a school assembly, when you had to recite a poem, or before a test, the result of which was supposed to determine your semester grade. The next stages of life revealed new dimensions of fear: during the final exams, before the university entrance exam, which was to decide about our future; fear of rejection of feelings when we fell madly in love; fear for loved ones; fear of life-saving surgery; finally: before death. Some were so afraid that, fearing that their lives would end, they never began to live - they took refuge in hiding places, and safe niches, and did everything not to have to face reality.[Eibl-Eibesfeldt, I.,1970; Ekman, P., et al., 1969, Ekman, 2003]

The fear of change comes from uncertainty, an internal belief that we will not be able to cope with certain events, and face circumstances that are unpredictable and indeterminate (this is where the fear of the future comes from). Fear means a lack of belief that we can cope and that we have enough strength to overcome possible adversities. Finally, fear may result from a specific personality trait and characterizes people who do not dare to change their lives, preferring to occupy a safe niche rather than risk failure or loss. Although excessive risk and bravado are not always advisable, people who are afraid to take them will never live life to the fullest, derive joy and pleasure from it, and will never expand their horizons of thinking, evaluation, and knowledge. Occupying a narrow, yet warm, hollow limits and narrows the views, making the world monotonous and one-dimensional. Living a full life means freeing yourself from the yoke of fear that blocks and limits you. It means shedding the armor. Of course, by shedding our armor, we become naked and defenseless, susceptible to blows, severe wounds, and scars.

However, only those who are willing to do so enjoy life to the fullest, discover the best flavors, and experience the most wonderful moments.[Eibl-Eibesfeldt, I.,1970; Ekman, P., and Friesen, W. V.,1971, Mathes, E. W., and Kahn, A., 1975]

Fear is needed for the body to mobilize possibilities and cope with potential threats. When we see a threatening and growling dog, we take action because we feel like we need to save ourselves. However, the problem arises when we are afraid, even though there is no threat to us, no danger awaits us. And even though we are aware of it, we react the same as if we met a mad dog on the road. Physiological reactions are then immediate: the heart beats like crazy, we feel cold sweats, our stomach tightens, our head hurts, our hands start shaking, our voice trembles, almost all muscles contract, we feel short of breath, and intestinal disorders cause diarrhea. Even though at the rational level we know that there is nothing to be afraid of, at the level of feelings we are unable to cope and tame this destructive emotion.[Eibl-Eibesfeldt, I.,1970; Matsumoto, D., 2006]

Try it yourself!

Freeing yourself from paralyzing fear and the overwhelming feelings of anxiety and uncertainty associated with it is not an easy task, because it requires a comprehensive reconstruction of thinking and perception patterns. First of all, you need to get to know the essence of your fear - so start by analyzing the situation in which it appears, what symptoms it has, and what its effects are. Use the below as an example.

I feel scared when...	Symptoms of fear	The effects of fear
I have to speak in a room full of people.	My body trembles, a wave of heat washes over me, I want to run away or sink into the ground.	I can't speak coherently, I start stuttering and stuttering, I lose words, I can't swallow my saliva.
etc.		

Filling out the table allows you to show the face of your fears (things that terrify you, cause anxiety, overwhelm you, torment you). Perhaps when you have finished listing the sources of fear, you have concluded that these situations are completely harmless, that the punishment is not the scaffold or the guillotine. Look at it this way and gain perspective. It often happens that fear has no real justification and no basis in reality - you are afraid of events that only seem dangerous, because - according to the saying - "Fear is scary" or "Fear has big eyes". Once you realize that your fear is a colossus with feet of clay, ask yourself what is the worst that could happen if everyone around you realizes that you are afraid. Will they laugh at you? Will they criticize? Will they mock you? Or maybe they will understand and see a human being in you…

Anger

A person's behavior that admonishes and later speaks nicely to the victim, on the one hand, may be a sign of a personality disorder, and on the other hand, a deficit in the most basic social skill, which is dealing with anger. Such a person lacks an important component of emotional intelligence - empathy. That person is unable to imagine being on the other side, i.e. in the place of the person towards whom he reacts with hostility and anger. Expecting others not to hold it against her after a tantrum, to erase her behavior from their memory, or to ignore her insults and curses shows an extreme lack of maturity and self-centeredness.[Eibl-Eibesfeldt, I.,1970; Koole, S. L., Veenstra, L., Domachowska, I., Dillon, K. P., & Schneider, I. K., 2022]

As an emotion, anger is a sudden, usually unpleasant feeling of annoyance, resentment, or rage. Nonverbally is shown in jaws tensed to a biting position as in sneering, postures of broadside display such as hands on hips, cut-off and head-jerk cues, frowning, tense mouth expressions, growling voice tones, and staring. Anger is responsive to and reflects visceral gut feelings because its muscles are mediated by the vagus nerve, which is a special visceral cranial nerve. [Eibl-Eibesfeldt, I.,1970; Coker, D. A., and Burgoon, J. K., 1987; Burgoon, J. K. 2018]

In the human face, corrugator supercilii muscles blended with occipitofrontalis and orbicularis oculi draw eyebrows down, producing vertical furrows above the nose. At the same time, procerus blended with occipitofrontalis produces horizontal wrinkles over the nasal bridge.[Eibl-Eibesfeldt, I.,1970; Ekman, P., and Friesen, W. V., 1971; 1975]

Try it yourself!

If you tend to get angry, if you cannot cope with the mounting anger or irritation that floods you, if those around you turn away from you because of your arrogance and arrogance, if you seethe with anger over the smallest things, then you should make an effort to change. You can deal with anger, like any other emotion, by learning about its structure and how it works. To do this, complete the following statements:

I am angry when.. ......
If I get angry, I start ....
The victims of my anger, i.e. the people on whom I release my frustration, are most often: ....

As you do this exercise, ask yourself if you have ever behaved in a way that makes you angry. How would you perceive and think about people who reacted the same way as you when they were angry? Did the victims of your anger deserve the way they were treated? How would you feel if you were in their shoes?

Exercise
When you are boiling with rage
Go outside, preferably to a park, meadow, or secluded place. Recall incidents when you exploded with anger, were angry, agitated, or fell into a passion. Recalling those situations, express your anger in a non-verbal way (not through words, but through gestures, facial expressions, body movements). Don't feel embarrassed or limited, just use your body to manifest the power of emotional upheaval. Express said rage for about five minutes. Then sit down and say how you feel. What's left of the rage that recently consumed you?

Whenever you feel even a little irritated, remind yourself of this exercise, and especially of the conclusions you came to after doing it. This way, you will realize that anger, even though it initially seems all-powerful and insurmountable, is a temporary state, and the reasons that cause it are trivial and of no importance.

However, what to do when it is not you who is angry, but someone else's anger affects you and you become a victim of frustration? In this case, you should behave rationally and not be provoked - that is, do not react similarly. Remember that only a rationalized reaction will allow you to immediately tame the bully, and may even make him feel embarrassed about his behavior. If someone gets angry and you are the direct or indirect cause of it, try to stay calm and become a mirror reflecting the other person's image. Identify his emotions and assign specific names to what he does. For example: "I see that you are angry with me, but most of all with yourself. You react very violently, you shout, you curse, you curse. Your face is red with anger, contorted with nervousness. Anger blinds you completely, and makes you call me rude, mean, and perfidious. When you say this, I feel sorry because these words are painful and unpleasant for me, they hurt my feelings. How would you feel if someone described you like that? I try not to hold a grudge because I imagine it's difficult for you, you can't cope with your problems, and your needs are not being met. I know you need attention, recognition, and support. But remember, getting mad at me won't change anything. "I'll leave you for a while, think about your behavior."

Depression

Depression is considered the bane of modern times. In its extreme form, it is particularly severe, causing numerous psychosomatic ailments, and if left uncontrolled, can lead to death. This concept is often overused, especially to convey poor well-being, but sometimes people do not realize that they suffer from depression. To find out whether the condition that is bothering you is depression, please refer (by answering "yes" or "no") to the following questions:

› You can't sleep, you wake up at night.

› You lose your appetite and lose weight despite not dieting.

› You are over-stimulated or, on the contrary, you lose strength and become weaker.

› You feel exhausted even if you sleep all day.

› You lack the motivation to act.

› You have trouble concentrating, your thoughts are racing and you sometimes forget about certain things.

› You see everything in black.

› You have been in a bad mood for a long time, you are

irritable.

› You feel worthless and hopeless.

If you have been experiencing most of the symptoms of depression presented for a long time, you should try to overcome it.

Depression is a serial killer!

Depression, like all other debilitating emotions, can be tamed. This is a difficult task, it requires determination and a true will to win. Take small steps:

1. Try to do as many daily activities as possible, such as: getting up early, taking a shower, preparing meals, shopping, going to work, taking clothes to the laundry, etc.

2. Think of and plan many additional tasks and activities you could pursue, such as learning a language, gardening, singing in a choir, yoga, aerobics, or other physical exercise, and writing a novel.

3. Fill each moment so that you do not think back to the events that triggered your depression. Remember that boredom increases the feeling of depression.

4. Create a space where you feel good and comfortable - change the decor of the room, buy new curtains, and put a bouquet of tulips on the table.

5. Try to go out to people or invite your friends, cook something tasty, drink good wine, talk. If you don't feel ready to socialize yet, don't force yourself, give yourself time. However, be careful not to isolate yourself for too long.

6. Try to control your sleep; if you would like to sleep all day - wake up and go to bed at a regular time; if you can't sleep - contact your doctor or pharmacist, take a walk before going to bed, eat light meals.

7. Pleasure yourself. Be good to yourself.

Shame

Shame is one of the most difficult emotions to work through. Working on shame is primarily about awakening self-awareness (which is tantamount to deepening knowledge about oneself) and developing an almost detective-like ability to find the real causes causing the feeling of shame or embarrassment. Most often, the source of this emotion is a false pattern of thinking about oneself, which includes the following statements: "I'm not worthy of something, I'm not good enough, I'm different from the rest." By being ashamed of yourself, something, someone or for someone, you trigger a false pattern of being less valuable - worse, stupider, uglier.[Matsumoto, D.,1991; 2017; Ekman, P., 1999;]

As an emotional cue, shame is usually an unpleasant feeling of disgrace, embarrassment, guilt, humility, or withdrawal that may be accompanied by some or all the nonverbal signs: cut-off, gaze aversion, hand-behind-head, eyebrow-lower, narrowed chest, slumped shoulders, shoulder-droop, shoulder-shrug, verbal pauses, and vocal grains.[Keltner, D., 1995; Eibl-Eibesfeldt, I.,1970; Ekman, P.,1999; 2003]

Try it!

Write down everything you are ashamed of and what embarrasses you. Then, by drawing arrows to the side, try to discover the key belief that makes you feel ashamed. Once you come to this belief, ask yourself if it is really a quality that sets you apart from the rest and that only you lack.

E.g. I am ashamed of my body. $\rightarrow$ I think I'm fat and unattractive. $\rightarrow$ I'm not perfect.

Am I the only one who isn't perfect because I don't have perfect measurements?

Shame, like most emotions, has two sides: positive (it is an indicator of our humanity - only animals and psychopaths are not ashamed) and negative when it paralyzes, overwhelms, intimidates, and limits. Anthropologically speaking, shame comes from violating a taboo or sacrum, i.e. a prohibition or sanctity applicable in a given culture. The embarrassment, disgust, and defeat that appear then indicate that we have behaved in an inappropriate or even unacceptable way. This function of shame is important and evolutionarily sound. However, feeling shame when we have done nothing wrong is wrong and destructive.[Keltner, D., 1995; Tracy, J. C., and Matsumoto, D.,2008] So whenever you feel ashamed, ask yourself if you have done something wrong or hurt someone. If not: why are you ashamed?

When tackling destructive feelings of shame, try to:

> accept yourself as you are;

> know that you can change many features (character, appearance, behavior);

> remember that you are not responsible for what was not your choice and did not result from a conscious decision;

> realize that in addition to your weaknesses (those you are ashamed of), you also have strengths (those you can be proud of);

> See that the things you are ashamed of are not a reason to be ashamed in the opinion of others;

> treat as a dogma the fact that no one is perfect.

Anxiety

Anxiety appears in a situation of uncertainty - when achieving a goal that is important to us is in question and the expected solution turns out to be questionable or not obvious. Anxiety is uncertainty related to the fact that we have no absolute influence on reality, that it is getting out of control, and can be surprising and unpredictable. It appears especially in matters that determine success and victory. An extreme sense of anxiety is depressing - it takes away your ability to act, it paralyzes you, which may ultimately lead to failure. Therefore, skillfully dealing with anxiety is essential to complete the work.

Anxiety is a mixture of fear and anticipation. Anticipation in this context means waiting for something that is of value to us in a symbolic or material sense (e.g. promotion, wedding, trip, job interview, competition for a position). The more important the issue, the more fear we feel. Anticipation itself usually does not cause discomfort, sometimes it even fills with excitement, because possible success opens up new paths and possibilities (when we anticipate, we want quick fulfillment). Anxiety becomes unpleasant because its second component is fear, which increases the possibility of failure and the possibility that the matter will not go well. Anxiety is a situation of a kind of duality: on the one hand, we are waiting for something, and on the other, we are afraid that everything will fail, so we withdraw or stay stuck. We should get used to fear because in life no one will ever give us a hundred percent guarantee of the desired outcome. However, the point is to place the accents differently - to mute the fear as much as possible and to emphasize the excitement that will give you wings and give you the strength and energy necessary to overcome the obstacles standing in the way of success.[Dijk, C., Fischer, A. H., Morina, N., Van Eeuwijk, C., and Van Kleef, G.,2018; Watson, N. M., Wells, T. J., and Cox, C., 1998]

To reduce anxiety about something that is about to happen and that you are not sure will go your way, focus primarily on the benefits or gains that the expected event will bring. So if you feel afraid of changing your job or place of residence, think that this change will result in establishing new contacts, the possibility of promotion and earning extra money, meeting interesting places and fantastic people. Enjoy it and don't think that you will fail (there will always be time to contemplate failure). To increase your excitement level of anticipation, try a visualization technique - imagine that everything turned out great, just as you expected. Think of the great joy and satisfaction that can come to you then. In your emotion organizer, write down what you're likely to feel.

The basis for reducing anxiety is unwavering self-confidence and the resulting proper self-esteem. If you don't believe in your abilities, question your sense of agency, constantly worry, and engage in negativity - you will most likely never realize your dreams or achieve your goals. Without fully believing that you have the potential to achieve the success you desire, and without believing that you deserve the best, you allow fear to dominate your thinking and behavior, which in turn will cause you to reject possible victory on a more or less conscious level. , you will withdraw.

Exercise
Believe in yourself and take the reins
Write down what features (values, attributes) you think characterize a person who is self-confident but not conceited, convinced of his/her value but not prideful. Use a three-column table to complete the task. In the first column, list at least 10 traits that show self-confidence. Next, write how you understand these features and what are the obvious indicators of their occurrence. Finally, in the third column, diagnose whether you have a given

feature and, if not, why you lack it.

Characteristic	Feature indicator	Occurrence
1. 2. 3. Etc.		

All people feel fear and anxiety, but for some people, these emotions are transformed into a state of mind, a kind of modus vivendi. These are morbidly anxious people, afraid of almost everything, who will always find a reason to feel afraid. They have a specific personality trait where there is a tendency to worry, depression, panic, or - on the other hand - they are people who are highly success-oriented, striving for perfection and being perfect.

'Nothing human is alien to me,' means you don't have to be flawless or perfect

Remember that you can make mistakes... you should because they teach more effectively than good advice or dry tips. So when you make a mistake, own up to it, learn from it, and start again, smarter. Instead of harsh criticism or reprimand for a mistake, think - based on the experience you have gained - how it would be better to behave in a given situation, and how to improve it, improve it.

What am I reproaching myself? What am I scolding and criticizing myself for	How can I improve this, just make it a little better?

Aggression

Aggression occurs in the world of people, animals, and plants. As Charles Darwin noted, aggressive behavior in the animal kingdom is the result of natural selection, especially sexual selection. Aggression, according to evolutionists, is a consequence of the fight for existence and survival (competition for access to food, water, territory, and females). Observations of animals behaving aggressively allowed us to create theories of reference to the human world, and thus to isolate the neurobiological and sociobiological mechanisms of aggressive behavior.[Takahashi, A., & Miczek, K. A., 2014] In this way, the theory of the instinct of aggression was created, which assumes that aggressive behavior is controlled by internal strength and results from the need to satisfy the fighting instinct. The creator of this theory - Piotr Bovet - observing fights among children and adolescents, stated that these fights do not result solely from external conditions (environmental or situational), but are a consequence of psychobiological dispositions, also known as drives. Bovet sees aggressive behavior as a component of human nature: "The vast majority of children aged 9 to 12 seek out fights for the pleasure it provides them, fighting is fun for them". The instinctive nature of aggression was also confirmed by the research of the Austrian ethologist Konrad Lorenz, who showed that aggression is an innate feature of living organisms, triggered by the self-preservation instinct that determines the organism's survival in the environment. Lorenz's discovery, honored with the Nobel Prize in the 1980s, proves that aggression is a beneficial phenomenon and a permanent element of animal (and therefore human) life.[Bernaras, E., Jaureguizar, J., & Garaigordobil, M., 2019]

Aggression is an antinomic phenomenon: in addition to the defensive and protective functions that guarantee the survival of the individual in the environment, it is a destructive mechanism that threatens the health and life of the individual. Aggression means harming someone, causing someone pain, attacking or assaulting someone, behaving in a hostile, aggressive, brutal or dangerous way. Aggression has many forms and manifestations - from the most extreme, when the aggressor is a ruthless murderer or an unpredictable psychopath, to slightly milder and more common ones, when a drunk husband starts a domestic fight, a teenager beats a friend, a boss mobs an employee, a high school student bullies a peer. Aggression is not only physical violence, but also toxic messages, accusations, gossip, and invective; in short: words that hurt, humiliate, offend and sadden are also aggression. There are several types of aggression and many specific forms. A distinction is made between: physical aggression (beating, physical abuse, corporal punishment), verbal aggression (ridicule, quarreling), transferred aggression (directed towards objects that are not the cause of aggression), symbolic aggression (having a substitute form in the form of satire, ridicule, ridicule).[Hart, S. D., Hare, R. D., & Harpur, T. J., 1992]

Aggression is most often defined as an intentional action aimed at causing physical or mental harm to someone. It is hostile and violent behavior accompanied by the appearance of characteristic mental states, such as anger, anxiety, irritability, dissatisfaction, sense of threat, emotional arousal, anger, fear, and hatred. Negative emotions are most often directed at other people or objects - resulting in the desire to destroy these objects or harm other people[40]. Albert Bandura and Richard H. Walters point out that aggression (like most pathological behaviors) may become a learned response to a state of physical or emotional tension. In this case, aggressive behavior is instrumental and is a means of obtaining a desired good or getting rid of something unpleasant.[Beryce W. Maclennan, 1961]

The operation of the aggression mechanism is well illustrated by the experiment of Anthony Doob and Larraine Wood. The researchers designed an experiment in which the experimenter humiliated and humiliated the subjects. Then the participants of the experiment were divided into two groups: members of one group had the opportunity to take revenge on their tormentor by administering electric shocks to him; members of the second group were deprived of such an opportunity. It turned out that subjects who had a chance to retaliate administered a moderate amount of shocks to the tormentor without feeling the need for further punishment. However, the respondents who could not "get back at them" were inclined (at the declarative level) to severely punish the one who humiliated them. It is therefore clear that the intensity of aggressive behavior and the will to retaliate depend on the individual's personal belief in "getting even."[Doob, A. N., & Wood, L. E., 1972]

According to some theories, aggression is always preceded by frustration, which usually causes aggression. Frustration is a state of deprivation when an individual is denied access to goods that are attractive to him - it is greater the more unattainable the goal seems and the higher its value. Frustrations are harmful because they are cumulative, so they "add to each other to produce aggressive responses of greater strength than would normally be expected from the frustrating situations immediately preceding the aggression."[Worcel, S. D., Shields, S., and Paterson, C. A., 1999]

All people had experienced aggression at least once when someone took out their anger or anger on them or tried to force them to do something. Most people also have experiences in their lives when they were aggressive - they raised their voices at someone who wanted to hit them or directed their aggression at some object.

Self-analysis of aggression

Recall a situation in which you experienced aggression (someone shouted at you, insulted you, called you names, tried to hit you or hit you, maimed you, forced you to do something, blackmailed you, threatened you, intimidated you, manipulated you). What feeling did it trigger in you? How did you feel about yourself then?

Form of aggression	What did you feel?	What did you think/How did you behave?

Aggression causes bad emotions (sadness, pain, hatred) and makes you think of yourself as less valuable, sometimes to such an extent that the victim of aggression (violence) takes the blame for the aggressor's behavior. Remind yourself of this exercise when your anger is rising and you feel like venting…

Hate

Hate is the most dangerous and destructive emotion. A man who hates acts of blindness is ready to commit the worst crime: kill in cold blood. Throughout history, there are known cases of acts fueled by hatred - genocides, persecutions, tortures, massacres. It is hatred that gives rise to stereotypes, prejudices, and, consequently, discrimination, unequal and unfair treatment of certain social groups - ethnic, religious, and sex. Therefore, hatred is the cause of racism, sexism, ageism, etc. This emotion consumes a lot of energy, which is why it destroys us first of all - the one who hates burns from the inside because, on the one hand, he tries to deny hatred (he internally realizes that hatred is evil and is a sin, therefore he tries to repress or replace it - e.g. by making sacrifices, donations), while on the other hand, unresolved hatred grows uncontrollably. Sometimes suppressed for years, it not only erupts during acts of hatred (rapes, murders, violence, quarrels, quarrels) but is also visible in the way people experience old age - people filled with hatred cannot come to terms with their age, they curse and curse people, they do not respect people that offer them care and help. However, a person who loved and was loved experiences old age calmly because he is aware of a life well lived.[Stephen K. Rice, 2009; Marazziti, D., Veltri, A., & Piccinni, A., 2018]

Hatred towards others appears when we hate ourselves or our lives when we cannot accept the situation we find ourselves in, and when we despise the gifts of fate. Hate is a wide range of emotions arising on the border of frustration, anger, jealousy, and envy. However, self-hatred can take essentially two forms: from masochism (inflicting suffering on oneself, putting oneself in the position of a victim), ending with sadism (when a more or less conscious pleasure comes from watching another person suffer, "enjoying" other people's pain, deriving internal satisfaction from observing difficulties and problems that concern him). It often happens as a reaction to the inability to cope with a certain situation - e.g., unable to cope with my responsibilities at work, I begin to hate my boss, attributing several faults to the individual. When I see that my neighbor is living a happy married life while I am getting divorced, my hatred towards her intensifies.[Jessica L. Tracy , Joey T. Cheng , Richard W. Robins & Kali H. Trzesniewski; 2009]

Fighting hate is very difficult because it is an emotion that is extremely resistant to change. It resembles a weed that has become so deeply embedded in the soil that pulling it out by the roots requires considerable effort and even additional treatments or tools. The first step is to become aware of the hatred rooted in us and admit that we hate something or someone. When you become aware of your hatred and see how much of it there is in you, how much it surrounds you, how much it draws you in and makes you addicted, you will begin to understand its mechanisms and distinguish its forms.

From details to the whole

It would certainly be difficult for you to answer the straight question: who do you hate? You would probably immediately deny the existence of the object you hate. Shame, or perhaps an overinflated superego, would prevent a true answer. Perhaps you consider yourself a walking perfection that abhors hatred, perhaps you consider yourself too holy to fall so low. Nothing could be further from the truth. So recognize that the hate is within you. To see how much of this feeling you carry within you and how much it controls you, start by analyzing the micro-manifestations of hatred. Using the thread-to-ball technique, discover who or what is the object of your hatred. Please refer to the following questions:

Name the people you have called an insult/curse in the last month.

....

....

Name people in trouble (they lost their job or property, got divorced, got sick, etc.) about whom you thought: "Good for them", "They got the punishment they deserved", or "Their pride was punished."

....

....

What do you hate about others? What human behaviors or actions drive you crazy?

....

....

Who and what do you envy?

....

....

Assuming you answered the above questions honestly, you can pinpoint the people who have become the objects of your hatred with a high degree of accuracy. Now tell me why you hate them. Do they have something that you lack? Or maybe they have something that's in you but you can't integrate or accept it? If you get rid of or at least reduce the level of hatred towards other people, it will be easier for you to live in harmony with yourself. So make every effort to achieve victory in the fight against overwhelming hatred. Look once again at the objects of your hatred. Think about them with kindness and sympathy, awaken warm feelings towards them, and try to explain their behavior, even if it seems particularly out of place, perfidious, rude, or calculating. For example: if you hate Teresa because she badmouths you and gossips about you, take into account her difficult life - staying in an orphanage, relationship with an alcoholic, lack of work... Once you notice this, it will be easier for you to look at her with understanding, and maybe even tenderly.

They hate people who have been wronged, full of complexes, and with low self-esteem. They constantly fuel the harm they carry within themselves because, in a sense, they are addicted to it - it gives them an illusory sense of uniqueness, of being different from everyone else, they are convinced that such harm that has befallen them has never happened to anyone else. These people are filled with regret, bitterness, and anger at themselves and the entire world. In the face of someone else's success or success in life, they realize that they have wasted their own lives. They constantly feel treated unfairly. Seeing enemies everywhere, they repeat like a mantra: "The world is evil and people are mean", "You can't trust anyone", "Life is hard and full of traps", "Others are waiting for me to stumble", "Man is a wolf to man". ..

There are many factors that can cause and fuel the wave of hatred. Most often, these are people or events that are beyond our control, over which we have no influence, and therefore we are helpless and defenseless towards them, and sometimes even completely dependent on them on the mental, physical and economic level. A husband begins to hate his wife when she cheats on him, because he still cares about her, because he still loves her. If this mental (emotional) dependence did not exist, the betrayal would be indifferent to him and would not involve any major emotions. A wife begins to hate her husband if she is financially dependent on him and he scrupulously allocates her money, limits her expenses, and blocks access to her account. If this economic dependence did not exist, there would be no basis for hatred to arise.

Another factor is jealousy. When we cannot come to terms with the idea that someone has more, better, especially when - in our subjective opinion - they do not deserve it, a feeling of reluctance and unkindness arises, which ultimately turns into anger or envy.

Love

Much has been written about love. Poets, artists, and philosophers praise its charms in highly refined phrases, suggesting that it is the most beautiful and perfect feeling. Also, many heresies were stated about love, most of these 'LOVE HERESIES' being told by Pope Francis (Cardinal Jose Bergoglio). Love is difficult to define unambiguously, which is why it is most often described in a figurative, metaphorical way ("like fire burns everything", while lovers are "on cloud nine", and have "butterflies in their stomachs"). Those who love do not doubt that it is love, but they are unable to describe what this emotion is and where it comes from. All they know is that this feeling cannot be compared to anything else or expressed in words.

Love, although it can take on various types, forms, and dimensions, is a universally known emotion. It occurs in all anthropologically studied civilizations, regardless of historical eras, cultural differences, and dominant social, economic, and legal systems. Despite its universality, it is an emotion with its specificity and dynamics, which makes it impossible to explain its mechanisms by referring to general sociobiological or evolutionary findings. It is separate and unique from all other emotions. Sociologically speaking, love is a unique, unrepeatable, and irreversible phenomenon. Like death, it does not ask whether it may come, it leaves no time to prepare for its acceptance or cancellation. Whenever it appears, it is born for the first time; always starting over, questioning what has happened in the past as well as what the future may hold.[Twardosz, S., Botkin, D., Cunningham, J. K., Weddle, K., Sollie, D., and Schreve, C., 1987]

Man looks for love because he feels an internal need for closeness, full acceptance, understanding, belonging, and security. He needs a belief bordering almost on certainty that there is a person in the world he can always count on, who will not disappoint, who he fully trusts. Love is born from the desire for another person, the need to exist for him and through him, from the feeling of emptiness that can only be filled by someone's presence. This mechanism results from basic ontological assumptions, where You is a supplement to I. Reciprocity is the basis of love, along with intimacy, trust and commitment. Love excludes egoism, because it consists in being for others - as opposed to being for oneself. It means constant availability regardless of the circumstances, especially difficult or unfavorable ones. It is a constant readiness to help, give a hand, take care of you, restore your self-confidence, believe in someone, make them feel good and noble. A person who is aware that someone cares about him very much, that he is worth someone's efforts, endeavors and sacrifices, that he occupies a permanent and extremely important place in someone's heart, is a lucky person, generously gifted by fate.[Floyd, K., 2006b]

There are many types of love: romantic-erotic (between lovers), maternal, paternal, brotherly, platonic (devoid of the sensual element), and divine. Each of these loves differs in terms of the dynamics of development of the person to whom the feeling is directed, intensity and duration, and the (absence) of the sexual context. Love is a mixture of many extreme emotions and states. First of all, the positive ones: are joy, enthusiasm, euphoria, and excitement that result from the powerful charge of happiness that love contains. Secondly, negative: sadness, pain, suffering, and fear - related to the assumption that a loved one may be lost, that one day he may leave us. To see the emotional multi-components of love even more clearly, complete the exercise below.

Exercise
Take a look at your love relationships (current or past). From the catalog of emotions, write down in a table those that fall within the scope of the love you experience and are its main components. In the second column, define the indicated component emotions. And in the third case, indicate the context in which they appeared.

Catalog of emotions: delight, happiness, joy, verve, revival, enthusiasm, euphoria, excitement, sadness, pain, suffering, grief, fear, disgust, helplessness, aggression, anger, reluctance, hatred, frustration, pride, fear, disgust, unpleasantness, rejection, loneliness, shame, embarrassment, certainty, uncertainty, nervousness, exhaustion, agitation, humiliation, rage, relief, discouragement, jealousy, bliss, contentment, satisfaction, suspicion, disappointment, excitement, elation, ecstasy, surprise, withdrawal, confusion, anger.

Emotion name	Define the emotion	Context of occurrence

Some people feel sorry for themselves and claim that they have never experienced love. They ask "Why?", seeing the causes of this state of affairs in a toxic family home, a failed marriage, punishment for sins, and a thousand other misinterpretations. They usually fall into a thinking trap that leads to the belief: "I am not worthy of love" or, conversely, "No one deserves my love." Try to change this pattern of thinking about yourself and others. If you are stuck in the belief that you are not worthy of love, start by looking for exceptions (e.g. my mother and sister love me, so I cannot continue to claim that I do not experience love) and gradually expand the circle of these people. However, when you feel that you can't love anyone, look around and simply surrender to this feeling - it will (contrary to what you think) sort out your life and put you on the right track.

Disgust

As one of the basic emotions, disgust protects us against direct threats to life. In the physical sense, it warns against anything stale, spoiled, or that may contain dangerous bacteria or toxins. An unpleasant odor, a changed consistency of food, a strange, abnormal color, and an off-putting taste are warning elements that cause a feeling of disgust. When we eat unappetizing, spoiled food, the body identifies it as a poison and often eliminates it from the body in a violent way, including through vomiting or diarrhea. The experiences of disgust and revulsion that occur then make it possible to remember for a long time various signs that warn against trying to eat similar food again. We all probably have experiences when, despite our inner hesitation, we were tempted to eat a certain dish, and then, after being poisoned and suffering from gluttony, we shuddered with disgust for a long time even when we heard the name of the food we had eaten.[Sluckin, W. (Ed.).; 1979]

The physical causes of disgust are relatively easy to recognize - just throw away spoiled food, wash infected surfaces, and choose food more carefully. Introducing proper health-promoting patterns, such as frequent and thorough hand washing or rinsing dishes, protects against poisoning. It is more difficult to avoid mental or spiritual poisoning.

Disgust towards unworthy behavior that we have been a victim or witness of, such as fraud, mobbing at work, sexual harassment, loss of trust in parents or guardians, and difficult experiences with the opposite sex - lead to psychological scars that are difficult to heal. These experiences often become a source of unconscious disgust, projected onto other people. As with anxiety, you need to undergo positive therapy and accept the past. It has already happened, so resistance and denial make no sense. The next step is to verify whether patterns from the past still influence our lives. The gradual evolution of these patterns and small changes introduced into everyday life lead to the creation of new models of behavior that enable a life of harmony and fulfillment.[Soderkvist, S., Ohlen, K., and Dimberg, U., 2018]

Spiritual "contaminations" are the deepest hidden and that is why they are the most difficult to recognize and consciously change. Fear of a punishing, angry God, disgust of the disgusting behavior of people who should be moral authorities, shame, and fear of admitting one's sins can become the cause of unconscious design. disgust towards religion and even the meaning of life on Earth. Spiritual reasons, although invisible, evoke strong emotions because they concern the foundations of life itself. Hence, it is necessary to create your system of values and live according to it, and at the same time experience the unconditional love of God, the Universe, and the Absolute and an attempt to give similar love to all beings - people, animals, and even plants and minerals.

Disgust informs us about excess and defines the boundaries that are appropriate for us. When we overdo it, we feel bad, and this applies both to the physical sphere - eating, drinking, excess activity - and the mental sphere. Excessive stimuli cause aversion and the desire to fast or escape. The ancient Greeks proclaimed the idea of the "golden mean", stating that going to extremes leads to emotional instability, often uncontrolled mood swings in response to the same external situations, and moderation in all areas of life leads to internal and external harmony. Disgust forces a distance from which we can appreciate what is useful for us, what delights us, and what tires us or poisons us.[Stern, D. N., 2007]

We feel disgusted not only on the physical level. It protects us against toxic relationships and allows us to experience and check which of them are valuable and which are harmful. After meeting some people, we feel discouraged and weak, and we feel aversion to our next visits. This mental disgust is a subconscious protective shield.

How does disgust manifest itself?

▸ A grimace appears on the face, which indicates reluctance - the nose is wrinkled, the corners of the mouth are drooping, the lips are pursed, or, on the contrary, the mouth is open to expel the contents from the stomach ▸ The salivary glands are stimulated to increase the secretion of saliva (which is bactericidal)

▸ Nausea and vomiting may occur

▸ The body positions itself in opposition to the triggering person or situation

disgust or tenses up, getting ready to run away

▸ There is an unwillingness or inability to repeat the disgusting situation

Surprise

It is an ambiguous emotion that combines positive and negative, plus and minus signs. For some people, it may be perceived as a joyful surprise, and for others as an unpleasant surprise. Surprise breaks our habits and shows us a part of the world that we don't know and don't expect. It teaches us that it is necessary to constantly push boundaries. Surprise forces you to change your views, and thus contribute to development - both personal and that of all humanity. Sometimes he turns the world upside down or, on the contrary, restores the disturbed order.[Frank, M. G., and Ekman, P., 1993; 2003]

It is an emotion that precedes other emotions, hence its duration is very short. If it had lasted longer, it would no longer have been a surprise.[Ekman, P., 2003]

Surprise is perceived with fear by more conservative people, and with curiosity by people eager for impressions. You can't prepare for a surprise, you can't tame it. Because it happens very quickly, it does not give us time to make rational decisions, activate defense mechanisms such as denial or repression, or return to old habits. It breaks down internal barriers and pushes towards new solutions. [Hager, J. C., and Ekman, P., 1997; Ekman, P.; 2003]

How does surprise manifest itself?

▸ The eyebrows are lifted to reveal the eyes, allowing them to be wider

opening them

▸ Wide open eyes make it easier to increase the field of vision

▸ The mouth is open, allowing deeper breathing

▸ The body freezes for a few moments - it does not know how the situation will develop and what reaction will be appropriate

5 - THE TWO-STEP METHOD OF EMOTIONAL INTELLIGENCE

Learning emotional intelligence should start with a thorough self-diagnosis. You're almost done with this stage. Now it's time for practical actions aimed at repairing what is broken, failing, or not working at all. An emotional structure is an ordered structure in which each element must function reliably and play specific roles. If one of the elements, i.e. at least one emotion, is defective or insufficiently developed, the entire emotional structure will not be correct.

As you already know, emotional intelligence is one of the most important competencies necessary for proper functioning in society. It can be said with almost 100% certainty that all failures in various social relationships (marriage, parenthood, employment relations, etc.) are the result of insufficient development or lack of this type of intelligence. Unlike general intelligence (IQ), it is not innate and passed on in the genes, but is a skill that can be learned and trained. You have probably met a person at least once in your life who you would say is emotionally intelligent and internally well-organized. We use this term to refer to people who respect themselves and others, know what they want from life and go in that direction, and are rooted in the "here and now" - that is, they do not create illusions, do not immerse themselves in utopias or fantasies. Organized people are discreet and subtle, they are not interested in the private lives of others, they do not gossip about them, they do not judge, they do not judge, they do not put themselves in the shoes of others, because they know that they are not there and will never be there. Organized people are primarily interested in their own lives, so they make every effort to make it harmonious, good, beautiful, and valuable. They have a well-established value system to which they remain faithful no matter what. Despite their beliefs and worldviews, they fully accept those who think and feel differently, allowing the whole world to be as it wants. They cultivate a virtue called mindfulness - they accept what today brings them with attention and affirmation, instead of dwelling on the past or wondering about the future. Organized people do not have complexes and do not tend to constantly worry, pessimism, and rumination (persistent dwelling on past events). They do not feel the inner need to criticize, fight, humiliate, cheat, or deceive anyone. They do not confuse, do not enter into conflicts, do not participate in quarrels. They are open, honest, natural, and spontaneous. They live in harmony with others and, above all, in harmony with themselves.

Learning EI is about the internal arrangement, creating a strong and lasting emotional structure. You will probably ask how to do it. You can compare this process to putting together a puzzle. If you are determined and devote enough time, the puzzle will eventually come together, regardless of the level of difficulty and complexity.

Putting together the self requires a comprehensive rethinking of the self-image, and consequently - reconstruction of the concept of the Self-created over the years, which consists of numerous experiences, reflections, and transitions. The first step in putting the puzzle together is to look at the image you want to recreate. Create a new image of yourself in your imagination, considering the principles of being emotionally intelligent. Arrange yourself exactly the way you put together a jigsaw puzzle - having the picture in your imagination, add, one by one, the individual pieces, until finally a coherent whole, a perfectly composed picture is formed.

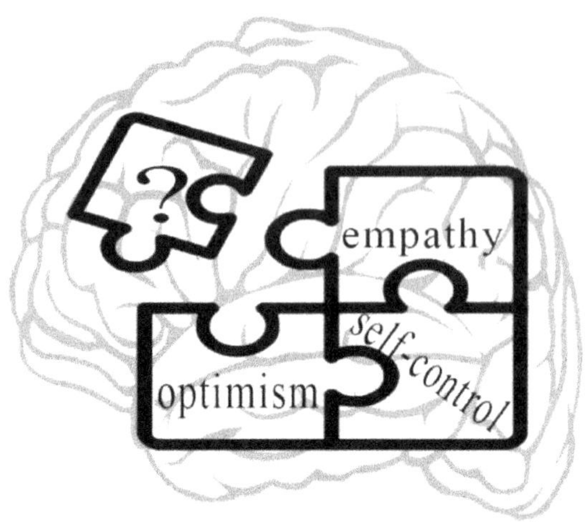

Emotional work, like any other type of work, requires a willingness to undertake it, to set conditions, to sign a contract, and a willingness to continue until the resolution, goal, or task undertaken is completed. You have to put a great deal of effort into the work, be committed and selfless, and, above all, recognize that a person - as a free and autonomous individual - is capable of influencing his or her life, shaping it according to the context in which he or she has come to function. Subjectivity and the causality that goes with it will enable effective and lasting change. However, you must independently and fully consciously decide that you want this change, reckoning with the many consequences - both joyful and unpleasant - of your choice. Know that every choice entails giving up something - you gain something, but you also lose something. An emotionally intelligent person knows that he can't have it all, and reconciles himself to this, not trying at all costs to keep what is not given or due to him. Nor does he make the level of his happiness dependent on his possessions.

Try it yourself!

A contract with yourself

The formal beginning of any work is to establish the terms of its performance and sign an agreement or contract. Use a similar model when working on emotions. In your emotion organizer, spell out as precisely as possible the terms of your work on yourself, i.e.: the due date (e.g., "On January 15, I will begin intensive work on deepening the relationships in my marriage"), the mode ("To improve self-discipline, I will get up an hour earlier and during that time I will run 2 km or at least exercise on a stationary bike"). Paraphrase this contract, taking full responsibility for your signature. Keep your word! After all, if you deceive yourself, how can you demand honesty from others?

First Step-Planning

The first step to change is to reflect on what you want to change, why you want to change it, and how you intend to do it. Reflexivity is a necessary and indispensable condition for any activity since only that which is carefully considered and analyzed in terms of gains and losses can be translated into actual strategies and actions. British sociologist Anthony Giddens points out that reflexivity, understood as awareness of what is happening, is an important component of identity. Through reflexivity, a person begins to ask the question, "How can I use this moment to change?" Reflexivity, finally, is the art of self-observation and reflecting on what you are feeling, what you are doing, what is happening now, what you are currently thinking about, and how you are breathing[46]. Instilling reflexivity is not an easy task, as it requires being honest with oneself, admitting one's mistakes, and seeing the fault in oneself. For many, facing themselves means quite a challenge, it is sometimes an experience so painful and painful that it becomes unbearable, which is why some prefer to lie or color reality (the strong sense of guilt that comes from realizing what we have done wrong, how much we have failed, could kill us). However, honesty with oneself has a cleansing and freeing power, which allows us to get rid of what is stifling and limiting us, and thus enables us to pick ourselves up from the emotional hole and move forward.

Confession

Confession brings catharsis - self-purification, i.e. liberation from sins, being above what is mundane or petty. Anthropologically speaking, it is a necessary ritual for a person to begin the process of inner transformation. So if you have decided that you want to change something in your life, confess it - to yourself and your confessor. As you probably know, the essence of confession is a sincere confession of sins, expression of remorse, and fulfillment of the required penance. When you meet these conditions, you can consider that you are starting over, anew - this time better and smarter. Reach for your emotion organizer. Write down all the things that bother your conscience and the spooky thoughts that haunt you. Then admit that what you did or said was wrong, hurt the other person, caused him suffering (it is important that you do not try to deny it, explain it, or minimize the pain you caused someone - just beat your chest). Now think if and how you could make amends, i.e. make the suffering you cause less. If you can, make amends; if not – resolve to never act that way again. The next step is penance (don't confuse it with PUNISHMENT!), which should be a fair reflection of the sin committed. To fairly assign yourself penance, stand on the other side - think what penance you would give to someone who would treat you as you did. Write everything down, set completion dates, and tick off completed "penitential tasks" one by one. Put yourself into it, don't treat tasks lightly. When you do the work honestly, stop blaming yourself - your sins have been forgiven. With this feeling, you can break away from the past. Drawing a line separating the past from the present is essential because you cannot start over again by being attached to what is irrevocably gone. You have to learn to close doors behind you. Don't worry about what happened and is over, don't go back and dwell on it. In life, you must constantly move forward, and abandon all bad emotions that make this progress difficult and make you feel sad, unfulfilled, resentful, and frustrated, which means you do not enjoy life and do not see its charms and splendor.

Now it's your turn. Present your postulates regarding your desired life model. In short, list what you want to be like (write at least 10 adjectives) and what it will give you, what benefits it will bring in interpersonal relationships, and what results it will bring when you become like this. Use the table below to complete the task.

How do I want to be?	What will I gain?

Setting the goal

The above exercise has made it a bit easier for you to determine the direction in which the change should go. Perhaps, having realized that some of your original assumptions did not help you and were therefore sterile and meaningless, you modified your vision of change. In outline, you know your goals and aspirations. So it's time to create a real goal list. To do this, find out how the goal should be formulated and what main elements it consists of.

In the process of creating and achieving a goal, the most effective method is the SMART method (the name is an acronym created from the first letters of English adjectives: simple, measurable, achievable, relevant, and timely defined), which defines the determinants of a properly set goal. So the goal should be:

› simple and clear - which means that the goal must be specifically named and clearly defined so that there is no doubt as to its meaning and interpretation - e.g. "I believe that my Achilles' heel is insufficient empathy, I want to work on it because I know "that this will make my social contacts less superficial";

› measurable, measurable - the goal should be measurable and verifiable - e.g. "When I expand my circle of friends to 10 people, I will feel that my level of openness and trust has increased significantly";

› achievable - i.e. realistic, possible to achieve by a given person, in a given place and time - e.g. "I am shy and introverted, so inviting a colleague from work for coffee will be a success for me";

› significant - valuable from the point of view of the person who pursues this goal, important and valuable, necessary for further development - e.g. "I want my husband to talk to me about his feelings, then there will be more understanding and mutual support in our marriage";

› time-bound - it is important to set a specific deadline for its implementation - e.g. "By the end of December, I will develop self-control, which will make it easier for me to fulfill my professional obligations on time."

Attention!

The goal must be as detailed as possible, taking into account all the above-mentioned elements. Above all, however, the goal must have specific guidelines - which means defining it well and making it make sense that is obvious to you. Take into account that the same concepts may mean different things to different people, e.g. for Roxeanne, being happy means being able to start a family and have three children; According to Clarisse, happiness comes from satisfying work, international contracts, and trips abroad. Therefore, when formulating your goals, write down how you understand them, what their interpretation is, and what meaning you give them. Be sure to also define what conditions you must meet to say that you have achieved the goal.

Goal	The meaning of my goal	How do I know when I have achieved my goal?

Measure your intentions

Avoid unrealistic or excessive goals, as difficulties in achieving them may result in discouragement, decreased motivation, and lower work efficiency. This regularity is confirmed by the Yerkes-Dodson law, which states that there is a close relationship between emotional arousal and the quality of activities performed - the higher the level of arousal, the greater the difficulty in performing the task. With this in mind, at the beginning of your journey, set yourself the simplest possible goals, the implementation of which does not dramatically exceed your actual skills, time, determination, and internal strength. For purposes of the so-called, there will still be time for the top shelf to be achieved.

Planning and acting

Working on emotions requires a detailed plan, which must include the following information:

› What emotions would you like to work through next, i.e. what is stopping you on your path to happiness?

› How much time do you give yourself to complete this task, i.e. complete the work?

› What work tactics will you choose, i.e. what methods and

techniques are you going to work with?

› What will you be like when you manage to overcome emotional blockages, difficulties, and limitations, at least partially?

Based on the information you obtained in the previous chapters of the guide, the exercises you performed, and your reflections based on the emotion organizer, you know your emotional structure. This means that you know what emotions dominate in your life and, consequently, what the consequences are, what they lead to, and what behaviors they cause. Remember that most emotions are complex, meaning that under one emotion there is a second or third emotion, and these are the ones you should work on. The key is to get to the deep foundations of each emotion. Only then can you begin the process of rebuilding your emotional profile.

It's time to put theory into practice. When planning the distribution of goals, keep order and moderation, do not impose a punishing pace on yourself, but move forward slowly and successively. Take another look at your list of resolutions and tasks to accomplish. Describe the individual stages of your activities in the organizer, and highlight what successes you achieved on a given day or what was a failure for you. The notes will help you precisely determine what emotional work you have already done and what you still have to do. Thanks to this, you will know what emotional situation you are in and you will see and understand the emotional mode to which you are subordinated.

The work, although tedious, will bring the expected results provided that you truly want a change and believe in your success. No matter how complicated your current life situation is, know that you can change it.

John and Monica had 2 children, and a beautiful home, in a few words, they were happy. Everything changed when out of the blue Monica informed John she wanted divorce because she found happiness with Klaus, and presented him with the papers to sign. John refused and in a few days, John was summed in court. Klaus accused John that he was maltreating Monica and her children. John lost everything: his wife, children, the house, and his job.

John retreated to live in his parent's old apartment. For several weeks John managed to live out of his savings (he intended to buy a Tesla). The situation worsened when he went to see his children, but his children rebuffed him 'Leave us alone you animal'. John became a heavy drinker. He had nothing to live for. His pain was intense. He hoped to kill himself by falling into an alcohol-induced coma. An ex-coworker, Stan went one day to see John, and when he saw John's condition, continued to visit him more often. During his visits, he left John several books about people who escaped depression and tragedy. After reading these books, John found out that he wasn't the first who was struck by tragedy. After Stan saw that John's condition improved, Stan decided to invite John out. After several weeks, because of Stan, John met Claudia. Because of Claudia, John regained hope and happiness.

If you are at a critical moment in your life and it is difficult for you to see hope on the horizon and believe that things can ever get better, accept the fact that:

› The world is not rational, anything can happen to you (including great happiness and the greatest misfortune);
› no person will always be with you and protect you from possible pain, suffering, and despair;
› A person can come to terms with loss and go through any trauma;
› no matter how much you suffer, the world will not stop, it will go on;
› Regardless of the dimension of the tragedy and the despair that accompanies it, you must return to the world of the living - do it for yourself and others;
› try to rationalize what happened, give meaning to the event that, like it or not, happened to you.

Best tactic

With clearly defined goals and a specific action plan, consider tactics that will enable the change process to be carried out effectively. The choice of tactic depends on several factors: which method is easiest for you, what types of emotional problems require working through, and what final assumptions are required. When learning emotional intelligence, it is best to use a two-dimensional approach focusing on both emotions and intellect, which is referred to by specialists as cognitive-behavioral.

The guide contains various types of empirically confirmed methods that open up a wide range of possibilities in working on emotions. They include both case conceptualizations and purely theoretical recommendations from which the proposed exercises are derived. Some of the exercises will be easy and pleasant, but others will arouse resistance and you will consider them unnecessary or boring. And put your greatest effort to accomplish the latter - what causes you trouble, what you react to with reluctance, what you strongly resist, affects the inner part of yourself that requires working through. There have already been a lot of conclusions and observations in the emotion organizer you run, so keep them in mind and come back to them as often as possible. Let organization and emotion management be the order of the day and become your natural practice.

To best practice emotional intelligence, use the reflective learning model, which involves processing every experience (especially those that are uncomfortable or unpleasant for you) through rationalized observation (i.e. one in which you turn off the subjective assessment of reality and focus on the facts sensory observable). Based on such observation, always try to draw specific conclusions, aim at generalizing reflection, and create new patterns of thinking and action. Then test these patterns in your daily, routine activities until they finally become automatic. Always put the acquired knowledge into practice, try not to skip anything, and don't think that you can skip certain elements of training - you need both a warm-up, proper training, and a final relaxation exercise.

Remember that it is not only about being able to understand the emotion but above all about being able to change it. The best means of achieving goals is the method of small steps - want progress (even minimal), not immediate perfection. Notice each step you take leading to your inner transformation. Reward your effort, even if it seems to you that it does not bring the expected and measurable results. Shape your life - it's yours from start to finish.

Action!

Having basic knowledge about your emotions, an established action plan, and selected tactics, start implementing your goals. The actions taken should be focused on three issues. First, start naming and defining what you feel and think about why you feel that way. Secondly, you need to get to the sources of emotions, i.e. diagnose what constitutes their basis, what causes them, and what factors determine their appearance. Thirdly, in relation to the above diagnoses, start modifying the scope and intensity of the emotions you feel, i.e. weaken them (if they overwhelm and limit you) or - on the contrary - strengthen them (if you are emotionally blocked and cannot feel or express the emotions that accompany you).

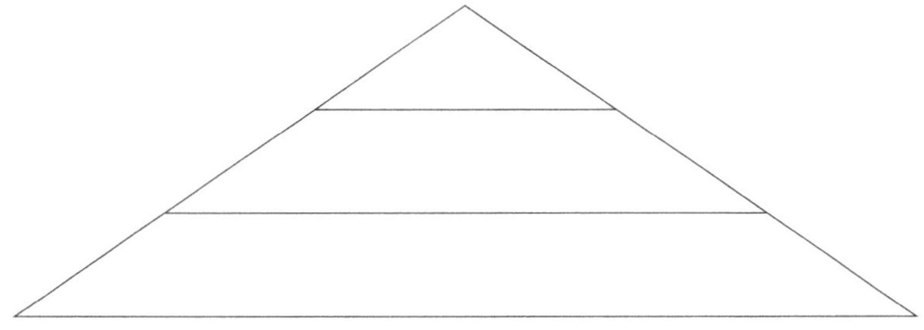

Notice and name what you feel

Sometimes it is difficult to focus on the emotion you feel and thus name what you feel. This is because emotions are multidimensional, many times complex, and sometimes too strong or too subtle to be isolated or assigned an appropriate semantic category. It often happens that they are contradictory and not obvious, so their categorization requires effort and great reflection. To learn to recognize them, you should become sensitive to every emotion that appears in you, even if its impact on your behavior or actions is microscopic. When you become sensitive to the emotional impulses coming to you, you will feel the relief of regaining control over your behavior. And that will be a real achievement!

It often happens that people block the emotions that constantly accompany them or deny their existence. The inability or inability to verbalize emotions (name what one feels) causes stress and mental dissonance, which increases the risk of identity rupture (the individual does not know who and what he is because he is torn by conflicting emotions). Verbalizing your feelings will help you discover the emotions you are experiencing. You will also be able to confront them with the socially accepted norm, which concerns whether they are consistent with experience and appropriate to the situation. Giving a name to an emotion is a preliminary condition for an in-depth analysis of the recorded emotional state. Naming reveals the emotion and, at least approximately, suggests what the individual feels, what is the problem and requires intervention, what brings satisfaction or, on the contrary, discomfort. When faced with the statements "I am depressed" versus "I am overjoyed", no one usually has any doubts about the subject's experiences and mental condition. Verbalization in interpersonal communication determines its effectiveness because when you define the emotion that is currently accompanying you (you say clearly and freely, e.g. "I feel fantastic", "I'm tense", "I'm depressed"), people around you will obtain clear information about your well-being. With this knowledge, they will easily adapt to the communication context and understand your (sometimes bizarre) reactions. The preliminary stage of correctly naming emotions is allowing them to occur. Become aware of your emotions, even if they seem inappropriate, out of place, ashamed, or afraid of them. Gaining awareness of your feelings and the ability to compare them, as well as refer to previously experienced emotions, in a personal dimension allows you to regulate and calm extreme emotional states (e.g. hysteria or panic). In the social dimension, however, it improves the quality of social contacts - people who understand the emotions of others and at the same time can communicate their own are more trusted, as well as more liked and respected. If you want to learn to verbalize emotional states, do the following exercise.

In the emotion organizer, plan the next three days, dividing each of them into regular time intervals (one hour, possibly two hours).

Systematically note what you felt during a given time, using the verb form "I am..."

(happy/embarrassed/sad/upset/satisfied/happy/concerned/frustrated /resentful, etc.). Next to stating what you are like, write down who or what made you feel this way.

First day Hours	I am…	Why?
06:00-07:00	unhappy	Unfinished yesterday's tasks
07:00-08:00	stressed	Possible reprimands
etc.		

Once you have completed the entire chart, take a closer look at how you usually are and what makes you feel this way. Consider whether you can reorganize your lifestyle in such a way that you don't feel stressed, frustrated, or angry so often... In addition, pay attention to whether the emotions you feel at a given moment are appropriate to the type of person you are - whether missing the bus is the real reason for being angry. Remember that every emotion you feel, even temporarily, leaves a lasting trace and determines your subsequent behavior towards your interaction partners. So if when you get out of bed you are angry at the whole world, this day will probably not be a good one. So when you declaratively declare: "I am...", try to place your emotion against the background of the general pattern of emotions, look at it from above, and treat it analytically and descriptively. You can do this as in the table below.

I am…	Concretely it means…
1. Sadness 2. Etc.	1. want to cry, you feel resentful, mournful, sad, filled with regret, with an inner feeling of emptiness... 2. Etc.

However, it may happen that you are not in touch with your emotional sphere, which is why you are unable to recognize your own or other people's emotions. This is a dangerous situation because it closes your perception of the outside world and prevents you from understanding people around you. So make an effort to learn to name what you feel based on your psychosomatic signs. To perform the exercise, use the side arrow technique, similar to the example:

My hands are shaking, my stomach feels heavy, and my mouth is dry. → I'm terrified.

I am constantly smiling and excited, I am filled with joy. → I am happy.

I blush, I look down, I don't know what to say. → I'm embarrassed.

Discover your emotions

Contrary to what we commonly think, we have no influence on most of the emotions we experience and express, they take place beyond our will and even imagination. This is because emotions are habitual - during socialization, we have been taught how to express them and which of them are appropriate to the situation. Neither the heart nor the mind is powerful enough to transform habitual emotions on their own because they are strongly encoded in the personality structure. On the one hand, this is a beneficial phenomenon because it frees us from the enormous cognitive effort that would have to be put into recognizing some event - e.g. if you had to wonder every time whether you should be happy when receiving a gift or whether you should respond to compliments with a polite smile, you would waste a lot of time and energy carrying out this mental transaction. So you react automatically. On the other hand, the habitual nature of emotions limits us greatly, sometimes even to the point that we do not realize what we really feel. In addition, habit means that we are unable to feel or show certain emotions - if parents do not teach a child to experience joy, he will probably never be able to enjoy or be happy in his adult life. Therefore, it is worth making the effort to transform the ossified personality structure and discover emotional depth.

To help you break down your emotions into their prime factors, use the onion diagram discussed below.

An onion is made up of many layers. To peel it and get to the inside, you need to slowly separate the layers. Suddenly cutting the onion across makes tears come to our eyes and we start crying. The same thing happens when working on emotions - if you want to discover the deep layers of your emotional structure too quickly and rashly, you may hurt yourself and it may be an unpleasant experience for you. So take a layer-by-layer approach.

Using some simplification, it should be assumed that emotions have a three-layer structure - they include the emotional core, the intermediary emotion, and the externalized emotion.

The first layer is created by an externalized emotion - visible, visible to the naked eye - e.g. a smile on the face, tears in the eyes, trembling hands, pulling hair from the head, biting nails. By looking at someone, we can classify them.

Depending on the context, the externalized emotion conveys a lot of important information worth taking into account in the interpretation of the emotional state, but you cannot stop at it alone. It is a shell of what is deeper.

Underneath the layer of externalized emotion, there is an intermediary emotion. As the name suggests, this layer mediates between the emotional center (core) and what we show to the environment. At this level, the process of modifying emotions takes place, which is conscious (we realize that we are not allowed to show real emotions - during business talks or negotiations) or subconscious (during socialization, we were taught to transform real emotions into others - socially approved, which are a simulation or ersatz of real emotions; when a child is angry, he lies on the floor and stomps - identical behavior in an adult would be unacceptable).

Finally, the deepest layer of emotions is called the emotional core - this is the core from which a given emotion originates, its basis, and its source. As the deepest layer, it is very difficult to indicate and define, because it is covered and sometimes tightly closed. All emotional work should be aimed at reaching the core, revealing and working through the central emotion that creates this core. The emotional core is formed in the early stages of life (childhood), it consolidates in its form over the years, which causes it to ossify. The emotions that constitute the core are very solidly built (sometimes even embedded) in the human emotional structure, which is why they are resistant to verification and change. In practice, the emotional core is the beliefs we have about ourselves. Sometimes we are aware of them, and we can point them out and give them a specific name, but more often they remain beyond the reach of cognition and self-perception. To put it more figuratively, they are buried so deeply that unearthing them requires the murderous work of emotionally clearing the rubble.

Try it

To reach the deep layers of emotions, start with the most external ones. So try to recognize and classify your characteristic (most common) external reactions - how you manifest your feelings. A set of unfinished sentences will help complete this task. Think about times when you experienced similar emotions and add the end of the sentence:

1. When I am filled with joy, I...
2. When I feel sad, I...
3. When I feel cheated, I...
4. When I'm afraid, I...
5. When something disgusts me, I...
6. When something amazes me and doesn't make sense to me, then...

Did you find it easy to finish the sentences? Did it cause you some difficulties? If you have had to think for a long time, you probably do not have a complete picture of yourself, you do not know how you react in the context of different emotions. So you need to become sensitive and focus on observing yourself. However, if you had no problem completing sentences, carefully analyze what you wrote. Next to it, write down how you would like to behave or how you think you should behave in a given situation. Designing alternative reaction models may seem like writing a science fiction novel, fantasizing completely disconnected from the actual situation, but visualizations trigger your imagination and cause an alternative scenario to exist in your head. The following exercise will make it easier for you to create alternative visions, and thus change the way you look and evaluate.

Exercise

Among the people around you, choose those who arouse

negative emotions in you (dislike, disgust, boredom, shyness, fear, anger, jealousy, and maybe even hatred), and imagine that for a moment you feel just the opposite towards them - like paradox: those you hate, you love.

Person	What do I feel	How do I behave in his/her proximity	The opposite emotion	If I felt this way, how would I behave?

Now take the next step and observe the cognitive motivations behind your emotional states. In other words, find out what thoughts these feelings trigger for you.

Answer the following questions:
1. When you are sad, what thoughts accompany you?
....
....
2. When you are happy, what thoughts accompany you?
....
....

Once you identify your threshold thoughts (often called automatic thoughts) that trigger your characteristic emotions, learn to control them. Focus on thoughts (and store them in yourself) that make you feel good or even great - thoughts of success. However, thoughts that are overwhelming, depressing, or lowering morale should be rejected or replaced with thoughts of success. If you want to break up with an emotion, create another one that will cover up or invalidate the first one. By practicing these changes for at least a month, you will be pleased to notice that it has become a habit in your blood and that thoughts of success have become habits (the programmed mind will work automatically). Get used to the new way of thinking about yourself and the positive emotions that result from it. Then you will see yourself in a new light. As Aristotle wrote: "We are what we repeat, and perfection is not a single act, but a habit."

To reinforce the art of replacing thoughts and seeing the glass half full, imagine the following situation: you work in a team of several people, and the work you systematically perform brings results, but you are still not sure whether the results are satisfactory to your boss. One day, your superior calls you into his office. The first thought that appears in your head is:

1. wants to praise me,
2. wants to reprimand me.

If you chose option one, you think well of yourself, keep it up! However, if you chose the second option, create in your imagination an alternative scenario corresponding to the first option. Staging will help you reformulate negative thoughts that are destroying your life (they lower your self-esteem, deprive you of self-confidence, and question your competence and talent). Recreate the alternative vision in your imagination several, or even better, a dozen times - until it becomes automatic.

Meet your needs

The starting point in developing emotional intelligence is awareness of your own needs. Many people are so accustomed to the fact that their needs are not met that they treat this deprivation of needs as a natural state that characterizes society in general. Meanwhile, you should realize or remind yourself that the needs you feel (both primary and secondary) are important and healthy, and you can demand their fulfillment. It's good if you are surrounded by people who fully and satisfactorily meet or help meet these needs. The problem arises when such people are missing (e.g. when parents are immature and do not understand what parenting is about, or what obligations arise from being a father or mother). Failure to meet a child's needs results in him, as an adult, choosing people - although he most often says that he "finds" them - who cannot give, and in extreme cases take full advantage and suck them out - they are emotional vampires.

Emotional vampirism is a psychological phenomenon that involves constantly and ostentatiously showing people your failures, frustrations, and poor well-being to gain their support and induce guilt, pity, and compassion. The emotional vampire, wanting to regain full strength and recharge internally, sucks the life energy from interaction partners. To achieve his goal, he cleverly uses methods of emotional manipulation: crying, spasms, threats, taking offense, putting on faces that arouse pity ("Let everyone see what a bad situation I am in"), stories about past illnesses, pain, or difficult home situations. Even short-term contact with such a vampire causes significant mental weakening and the transfer of sadness, tension, grief or blues, and even real somatic suffering.

The process of creating emotions is illustrated by the following relationship diagram. Look at it carefully.

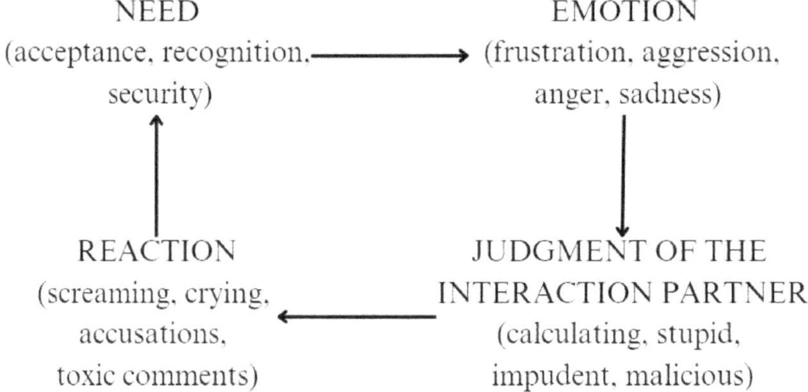

As you have noticed, emotions (especially negative ones) are triggered by unmet needs. To understand this relationship even better and see how this mechanism is activated for you, perform the following exercise.

Remember a time when you felt very bad and were filled with destructive emotions, and write down what need was not met, what you were missing, and what reaction you expected from other people.

1. When and under what circumstances did I feel bad? (Name the emotions that you felt.)

....

....

2. What was I missing then, when my need demanded fulfillment?

To further deepen your self-awareness of needs and develop the ability to reach them and reveal them under the guise of emotions, perform the following exercise - similar to the example given.

Exercise

Scheme of unfinished sentences:

1. I yelled at my child. → I found it disobedient. → I was frustrated. → The boss didn't appreciate my work and told me to change the project. → I thought I was hopeless.

2. I argued with my girlfriend/wife/husband. → .... → ..... → .... → ....

3.............................. → .... → .... → .... → ....

4.............................. → .... → .... → .... → ....

5.............................. → .... → .... → .... → ... .

The starting point in working on emotions is to diagnose what unmet needs lie beneath your emotions and the resulting reactions. If you know that your frustration comes from a deep but unmet need for praise, approval, or appreciation, you will be able to reduce your frustration level to zero by surrounding yourself with people who will satisfy this need. You can also achieve this – even more effectively – by learning how to appreciate and acknowledge yourself.

So if you want to change your emotions, change your needs, or start meeting them fully and satisfyingly. First, know your needs. Using the table below, the rate that is very important, important, or rather unimportant to you. Place an X in the appropriate box.

Need	Very important	Important	Unimportant
safety			
affiliation			
freedom			
acceptance			
recognition			
respect			
love			
closeness			

devotion			
sacrifice			
understanding			
honesty			
trust			
admiration			
appreciation			
being heard			

The information gathered in the table reveals the hierarchy of your needs. This knowledge is crucial because emotions begin with needs. Now take the next step and consider what needs you have that are unmet or only partially met, or certainly less than you would like. Of the needs listed in the table, list those that are met at 100%, 90%, 80%, 70%, 60%, etc. If your needs are met at 80-100%, you can consider yourself lucky. It is worse if they are not satisfied at all or the degree of their implementation ranges from 10 to 50%. Write them down and acknowledge that all destructive emotions come from them (hatred, resentment, fear, aggression, etc.). The dissatisfaction that you feel so painfully most likely has its origins in childhood and the parents' inability or lack of willingness or will to care for their child. Of course, you can't go back to that period, so now you have to find another way to meet your needs. Metaphorically speaking: imagine that you are hungry, you need a specific type of meal - prepare it as delicious as you can and satisfy your hunger. To learn to satisfy small and large hunger, think about what exactly you need and expect and what the components of each need are. An effective way is to create a recipe for respect, trust, acceptance, and other needs. Remember that you are preparing this recipe yourself.

Do It!

An emotional cookbook – a recipe for respect

Ingredients: a pinch of praise, a handful of words of appreciation, two scoops of words of admiration, a lot of acceptance – and compliments to taste.

Now it's time to implement the recipe - just mix the ingredients.

Stand in front of the mirror, look at yourself favorably and with approval, recall the compliments you have ever heard about yourself (someone found you intelligent, witty, appreciated your nice smile and thick, shiny hair); mention words of appreciation and praise directed at you (someone praised your self-denial and persistence in pursuing your goal). Write everything down, even if you consider it just polite nonsense.

Treat any other unmet need in the same way (create your recipe for love, trust, freedom, etc.). Some recipes will be difficult for you to prepare alone - so ask a loved one for help. After completing the exercise, write down any conclusions that come to your mind.

Collected conclusions:

....

....

....

....

....

....

....

....

Once you know what needs you have that need to be met, then you will recognize and understand your emotions. This is a necessary condition for the correction and compensation process. There are only two entities that can meet your needs: other people and yourself. However, it often happens that emotional disorders block access to people who can help you. You do everything to discourage them because they seem uninteresting and unnecessary. Let them come to you, open yourself up, and let them become part of your life. Then you will understand that they can fill the emotional hole that is inside you. The mechanism of self-fulfillment of needs works similarly. Think of yourself as an independent and autonomous entity with the power and resources to shape your own life. So take yourself seriously, become your authority, your first and basic frame of reference. Stop comparing yourself with others, caring about their opinion of yourself, while admitting your mistakes, and accepting flaws, shortcomings, or weaknesses. Maintain your self-esteem even when you are the target of harsh criticism or rejection. Remember: you have the right to live well and be happy. Appreciate your life, live it the best you can, and enjoy it. It is the greatest and only asset you have. And be sure that no one will give you this gift a second time, there will be no chance to experience it again.

6 - EMOTIONAL WORK!
DECIDE HOW YOU WANT TO FEEL!

Every person faces a choice in life: surrender to reality or shape it. Figuratively, it can be compared to the course of a river. Going with the flow is easy and pleasant, it does not require any special effort, and the river carries itself. However, it is extremely difficult to swim against the current - you have to row hard, flex your muscles, and wipe the sweat from your forehead. There come moments when you have had enough, perhaps you consider turning back, mooring, or interrupting the journey. You dream of peace, comfort, and rest. The heroic attitude seems unnecessary, ridiculous, and grotesque to you because you see that people acting on the line of least resistance are doing very well.

Shaping your life is a challenge, not everyone undertakes it. Instead, we involuntarily surrender to its course - we give up on our dreams, we stop looking for true and great feelings, and we settle for substitutes. We live in any way, thinking that there is no other way. Developing emotional intelligence will allow you to understand that you have a great influence on the shape of your life and you are responsible for it. So if it doesn't meet your aspirations and expectations, think about where you went wrong.

Your life is in your hands, you can do whatever you want with it. You can choose to be successful and happy, or you can choose to complain constantly and look for imaginary problems. Regardless of the choice you make, remember that you are the creator of your life, the one who decides where it is heading. You decide what your marriage, contacts with children, friends, and all other personal and professional relationships look like. You are the cause of your misfortunes, failures, and failures, regardless of where you are in life. And only you can change your life by starting to live better and smarter. Gather courage and take responsibility for your life.

To do

To find out whether you are determined and confident enough to change or modify your thinking about life and, consequently, your behavior, actions, and reactions, answer the following questions:

› Do you believe that you are primarily responsible for your life?

› Do you believe that you make the choice as to what direction your life is heading in and that you can change that direction no matter what?

› Do you agree that the way you feel is the result of your decision?

› Do you think you are responsible for your good or bad mood?

› Do you think you control your emotions and have actual influence on what happens to them?

If most of your answers were affirmative, you can confidently say that you are ready for a change and you know that it involves taking the helm, i.e. managing your fate independently and maturely. Being convinced that you have a real influence on what you think and feel, you can control actions and reactions that are derivative of your thoughts and feelings. However, if you answered no to most of the above questions, justify your answers - what facts or beliefs do not allow you to agree with this formula? Regardless of how you argue your opinion, know that only when you recognize your strength and agency do you have a chance to be who you want to be.

Working on emotions is about giving meaning to life by mindfully experiencing each moment. You will gain this skill by monitoring the activities you perform, planning them, summarizing them, and thinking about how they could be improved. Know that the effort you put into shaping your life will not be wasted. By making an effort and acting actively, despite mounting obstacles, difficulties, fatigue, and bad mood, you will achieve a state of mind in which nothing is impossible.

Face your emotions: don't deny them!

When working on emotions, remember a few key assumptions. First of all, the effects will be visible only if you look at your emotions honestly and sincerely and analyze them denotatively, i.e. as they appear, without additional interpretations, embellishments, or distortions. You must not deny or repress your emotions, because then you are lying to yourself, and the recovery plan and the work associated with it will fail. Second, most emotions are complex (involving two or more others), so emotional labor requires a comprehensive approach. You need to be patient and act on several fronts. Be a brave soldier. Despite the inevitable obstacles, do not desert, do not lay down your arms, and do not give up. Thirdly, and finally, even when you overcome bad emotions, do not rest on your laurels, thinking that your emotional intelligence is already at the right level and does not require further corrections or improvements.

The milestone is becoming aware of your own emotions and naming them, even if they are very bad. This, of course, requires great courage and breaking the taboo imposed by culture. So admit that there are times when you hate your children when you feel disgusted by your parents, when you despise yourself. Become aware of all your emotions, remembering that they may arise and that you have the right to feel that way. Negative emotions usually have a justification, they are in a sense true because that's how you feel at a given moment (sometimes you are hysterical, and from the outside, the situation that affects you and hurts you so much is of little importance). So you shouldn't deny your emotions (tell yourself and others that you don't feel that way), nor should you repress them (deny their existence). It is also important that you do not exaggerate the emotions you feel, do not fall into depression because of them, does not panic or catastrophize based on them, and do not dream up Dante's visions. Bad emotions are also necessary if only to see the good ones against their background. However, the essence of proper emotion management is proportionality and maintaining a healthy distance from what you happen to be feeling.

Catching the distance, what does it mean?

To gain some distance, you should understand that who you are and what you are like is not of concern to other mentally healthy people. They live their own lives and do not have to focus on other people's failures to increase their self-esteem. So take it for granted that even if for you the event was of great importance and you did not perform well (you think: "I made an idiot of myself", "I turned out to be a failure", "I behaved like an orphan", "I am trash"), for others, it mattered little or nothing - perhaps they didn't even notice. Don't take yourself too seriously, because despite what you may think, the world goes its way and doesn't revolve around you. You should distance yourself from yourself, which, paradoxically, will allow you to get closer to people. To look at your failures from a distance, use the scaling method. If something bad happens to you, something you blame yourself for, and you think it's the end of the world, put it on a scale of 0-100 (where 100 is the worst misfortune you can imagine, e.g. that you are terminally ill and two months to live).

$$0 - 5 - 10 - 15 - 20 - 25 - \ldots\ldots\ldots\ldots\ldots\ldots\ldots - 100$$

Exercise

An invitation to an emotional pizza
Imagine that you have a pizza in front of you, the main ingredients of which are emotions. Pizza is multi-ingredient, topped with a thick sauce composed of moods, and experiences that you have experienced. On a new page of the previously created emotion organizer, draw a pizza - divide it into many pieces corresponding to some stage of your life, e.g. childhood, early youth, university period, ongoing marriage, etc., and then mark each of them the main ingredients, i.e. the emotions that they dominated.

Recalling the taste of individual pieces of pizza, you noticed that each of them tasted different, each was seasoned with a different spice - more salty, sweet, or bitter. Nevertheless, you ate all the pieces, although some of them were certainly hard to swallow, they stuck in your throat and you wanted to regurgitate them - if you had known beforehand that they tasted like that, you would never have put them in your mouth. Some of them, in turn, tasted very good, the ingredients perfectly suited the palate, and tickled the taste buds, leaving a long-lasting memory of culinary delight. You would have eaten more of them, but they ran out. Sometimes it happened that someone helped you prepare your pizza, perhaps made it or seasoned it for you. Or instead of you, he decided what kind of sauce it would be covered with and how big the pieces would be. Regardless of what happened in your case, every piece you ate, even... even every bite, made you realize something, taught you something, and opened you to new, previously unknown flavors.

The pizza metaphor is intended to show you that life - like the mentioned dish - is divided into pieces (stages), which, although they are separate parts, form one coherent whole. And this whole thing is the most important, it counts the most. Although life is full of various events that have different flavors and bring different memories, you must accept that it all made sense, shaped your life, and decided that you are exactly where you are today. No matter what you think or how you evaluate the past, try to accept and accept your experiences, even if it was difficult for you to go through them and the bitter taste of defeat remains in your mouth.

It often happens that we are overwhelmed by the images of happiness and perfection promoted everywhere. The media, in particular, dazzle with messages according to which a person should always be joyful, smiling from ear to ear, free from worries and worries. He should be a successful person and look great: have a slim and firm body, radiant and flawless skin, thick hair, a toned stomach, or shapely hips. There are many determinants of physical beauty, and each new ideal of beauty created causes increasing stress and fear that we will never meet the challenge of perfection. Images disseminated in the media cause a feeling of disgust, helplessness, and, as a result, cognitive dissonance, which results from the feeling of difference between who we are and who - according to commercial messages - we should be.

Perhaps you are not resistant to popularized trends, perhaps you constantly accuse yourself of deviating from the ideal, or perhaps you think that if you were different, you would be happier. This way of thinking is harmful and disastrous, change it! Believe in yourself, appreciate who and what you are. You don't have to be perfect, you have the right to make mistakes, you have the right to be weak, you have the right to feel bad, you have the right to be in a bad mood, stressed, sweaty, and red. But you also have the right to take care of yourself, to mobilize for greater things! Break up with exhausting perfectionism but don't fall into carelessness, relativity, and laxness. You have the right to be yourself, you have the right to live.

Recognize it as an indisputable fact that you have the right to be weak, that you can make mistakes and fail. If someone demands perfection from you, he or she is probably mediocre and compensating for his shortcomings at your expense. Small and insecure people always do this, avoid them. Never blame yourself for doing something wrong; Don't blame yourself for not being able to meet someone's expectations despite your best efforts. You are not a cyborg! Mistakes, weaknesses, stumbles, and imperfections are the essence of humanity. Perfect people do not exist - everyone has flaws, everyone struggles with everyday problems, they suffer from colds, they are afraid and they cry at night.

Get along!

The preliminary condition for changing emotions (and therefore reactions) is accurate recognition of the thoughts activated by certain situations or certain people. If you can spot them and classify them appropriately (as negative or positive), you will increase your ability to control how you behave, and therefore how you are and how you present yourself to others. By guarding and controlling your thoughts, you will gain the ability to direct your life, take responsibility for it, and therefore make it what you want it to be.

Remember that destructive and dysfunctional emotions are deeply ingrained, and even when you think you have them almost under control, they may still resurface because they have been a learned model of how you respond and perceive social phenomena for many years. When interpreting reality (what happens to you, the behavior of those you meet), you refer to emotions that are known and available to you. Until you learn new emotions or adapt them to the context, you will keep returning to established reaction patterns. You need to realize that some (maybe all?) of your emotions are non-specific – that is, they do not correspond to the facts being interpreted. When you feel fear, it does not mean that you are in danger. When you feel ashamed, it's not because you're violating some taboo. When you are aggressive, you are very afraid.

My priorities	Why my priorities are important

Write down the worst self-descriptions that come to your mind, don't skimp on words. Then write down who else you think deserves the same label - they can be real or fictional characters. If you think about yourself: "I am furious" - then how do you describe the bloody dictators: Stalin, Hitler, Mao Tse-tung? And if you consider yourself a failure, what should you say about Forrest Gump? If you think you're ugly, what was Quasimodo like? Pay attention to the fact that your thoughts about yourself are biased, you exaggerate your shortcomings or flaws. Using the right arrow technique, try to weaken the power of the label you identify with and even derive something good from it, e.g.

1. I'm a jerk. → I'm acting stupid. → I am unreasonable. → Maybe I'm not down to earth and sometimes think about blue almonds, but that doesn't mean I'm an idiot.

2. .... → .... → .... → ....
3. .... → .... → .... → ....
4. .... → .... → .... → ....
5. .... → .... → .... → ....

On the other side of the mirror

The body, understood in sociology as a tool for thinking and acting, is a reflection of experienced emotions. Specialists in body language, non-verbal communication, and image creation have no problems determining what a person feels and thinks based on physical appearance. This is because it is almost impossible to control the body to the point that it communicates something other than what it feels. Each emotion is visible in facial expressions and/or gestures in a more or less clear way, simultaneously signaling the individual's internal state. When we are ashamed, our face turns red, we break into a cold sweat, and we look down; when we are afraid, our hands tremble, our legs become hyperactive, our heart beats like crazy, and our breathing rhythm changes. The descriptions of these somatic signs could be multiplied, because, let us repeat once again, all emotions are reflected in the body, which is an emanation of intrapsychic experiences and processes.

Somatization is one of the defense mechanisms (a way of dealing with internal conflicts) that confirms the close connection between the body and the psyche. Somatization involves the physical (bodily) experience of ailments that may herald a disease or indicate its existence. In reality, however, the body is completely healthy, and the phantom pains that occur have their source in the psyche (they result from a growing, most often unconscious, sense of anxiety, stress, and tension).

The relationship between soma and psyche is two-sided and directly proportional - not only do emotions profile body image but also body image influences felt emotions. Use this relationship when working on emotional intelligence. Start observing your body closely. This is an extremely difficult task because humans have no natural ability to look at themselves from the outside (only heroes of fantasy novels have a retractable third eye). You may think that you can skip this task because you look at yourself every day while shaving or applying makeup. This is about a different type of observation - one that is based on conscious and reflective looking. Of course, a mirror is an essential attribute, but in addition to it, look at yourself in store windows, in the mirrors of parked cars, in bus windows, literally everywhere you can. See your face in various social situations - going to work, jogging, standing in a queue at a store, dealing with matters at the office. Intimate observation is also necessary, in front of the bathroom mirror, consisting of contemplating the body in silence and peace.

Be your best friend!

Stand naked in front of the mirror. Look at yourself very carefully. Look at your own body from head to toe, almost inch by inch. Once you look back, treat your reflection as a new person to whom you can tell what you think about it, what feelings it evokes, and what your opinion is about its appearance, facial expression, and body posture. Talk about both advantages and disadvantages, shortcomings and weaknesses. Let the description be reliable, but also graphic - full of comparisons and references. When you turn to the person in the mirror, look into their eyes with understanding, acceptance, and warmth. Even if you say something unpleasant, say it gently, with kind words, so as not to offend her. Once you have finished the description, the person in the mirror will ask you what to do to make it better, to make it seem more beautiful, better, more perfect. And you have your answer...

Establishing contact with your body is especially useful when you feel internal dysregulation, which results from a lack of coherence between what is happening inside you and what is outside. If you are not aware of your body and do not know what it is expressing, it will be difficult for you to develop the basic component of emotional intelligence, which is the ability to self-reflect. The configuration of the body and mind allows you to work through difficult and painful emotions without compromising your physical and mental health. So try to monitor your body all the time, take care of it, respect it, and treat it with special gentleness. Make a habit of focusing on physiognomic reactions (both positive and negative), trying to find their causes or sources. You should be able to answer the question of when and why your body feels and looks great, and when it doesn't.

Try it!

Looking closely at the body, focusing during observation, and treating the body shell as an object of meditation will help you understand what is happening in your body and, therefore, in your mind. Write down everything that comes to mind when you think about your body in general and in its parts (face, arms, hands, legs, feet, hips, shoulders, neck, eyes, nose, mouth, etc.). Make sure the description is accurate and reliable.

› General description of my body:
....
....
....
› Characteristics of individual parts of my body:
....
....
....
....

What conclusions come to your mind after performing the above exercise? Do you accept your body fully, do you like it? Or are you rather dissatisfied with it, ashamed of it, disgusted by it, or maybe even hated? If so, tell me why. Then list at least six (realistic) possibilities to change your body image, and make it healthier and more beautiful:

1. I will eat healthily and 1/4 less.
2. ....
3. ....
4. ....
5. ....

Take care of your body, it is your best calling card. It conveys a lot of information about you - in a non-verbal way, it communicates whether you are at peace with yourself, disciplined, trustworthy, whether you value and respect yourself, and what emotions fill you from the inside. Your body is an excellent indicator of the condition of your psyche. So since it is so important (after all, it determines your existence - the fact that you live and move), approach it with sensitivity: do not torture it with draconian diets, do not subject it to painful procedures, do not experiment with it and on it, do not punish it by overeating starving yourself or starving yourself; working beyond strength or lying in bed all day; training and exercising until you drop or avoiding physical activity. Constantly observe your body and listen to it. It sends you many warning signals from within. Signaling fatigue and depletion of energy reserves, it demands rest, relaxation, rest, a moment of respite, and peace of mind. However, when you feel depressed, it indicates the need for some pleasure (eating a delicious dessert, staying in a sauna, getting a massage, taking a foam bath, etc.). If you ignore these signals and remain deaf to the voice of your body, it will rebel and become your enemy - you will start to gain weight, get ugly, get sick, your body will hurt, and become unwell.

If we cannot cope with stress, fatigue, and everyday problems if destructive emotions take over us permanently and we are not determined enough to change it, the body becomes a punching bag - we take out our frustrations on it, punish it, destroy it, and thus we deprive them of their dignity. If you tend to take out your frustration on your own body, change it. Start treating your body graciously as best you can. Give your body care, tenderness, and delicacy, and pamper them. Your body deserves it.

Feel your body...

Lie down on the floor so that you are fully flat on it, whether you prefer to lie on your back or stomach. Don't think about anything specific, don't let your mind be occupied by anything, and be free from worries and obligations for a moment. Stay alone with your own body, spend some time with it. Feel it whole and piecemeal. While lying down, think about individual parts of your body and at the same time try to press them harder against the floor so that - literally and metaphorically - you can feel them even better.

Acknowledge your face...

The face, and especially the eyes, are sometimes pompously described as the mirror of the soul. This poetic description is justified because the face expresses emotions, even if you try to hide them. Of course, some people can disguise themselves and put on a good face to play a bad game, but this is a task that requires great skill. Actors spend many years learning how to act with their faces, i.e. adapting their facial expressions to a given emotion, and only the best can create a convincing acting role. When working on the body, it is very important to profile the face, i.e. give it a certain expression, give it a face. Pay attention to your face –

outline it in your imagination and then describe it. Then look in the mirror and describe the face again. Compare both characteristics. Which description was more favorable? Why?

How you see your face in your imagination?	How do you see your face in the mirror?

Justification: ....
....
....
....
....

Emotions influence the behavior of the body (facial expressions and gestures), but they can also be different. To find out, try the experiment of creating inner joy through outer joy. Smile and adopt a cheerful expression, but without unnecessary artificiality or showiness, just focus on something pleasant and hold that thought. For the next few hours, try to keep your cheerful expression on your face; maintain a light, natural smile and keep it up – even if you lose the desire to do so. Observe other people's reactions to your face. Record your observations.

....
....
....

The case of Guillaume Duchenne

In the 19th century, the French physician Guillaume Duchenne distinguished two types of smiles. The first involves tightening the zygomatic and orbicularis muscles of the eyes, which results in lifting the corners of the mouth and cheeks, causing wrinkles to appear around the eyes. This smile is assessed as sincere, resulting from truly experienced positive emotions. The second type of smile is caused by the tension of only the zygomatic muscles. The mouth smiles, but not the eyes, which is why it is perceived by all stewardesses - hence it is called the Pan Am smile (an abbreviation of the proper name of Pan American World Airways, i.e. American Airlines).[Frank, M. G., and Ekman, P., 1993; Schneider, K., and Josephs, I.,1991; Galati, D., Sini, B., Schmidt, S., and Tnti, C.;

2003]

The next phase in taking care of your body is to become aware of which emotions have a positive impact on your body (under the influence of which emotions you look radiant, bursting with energy and vitality, you smile), and which ones have an unfavorable or rather extremely negative impact (you slouch, lower your head, face adopts a sad or unpleasant expression). To diagnose this, you need to conduct a systematic study of emotions regarding physical appearance. In your emotion organizer, plan the next seven days for body observation. It should be conducted in two dimensions, using two mirrors: the real one (you look in the mirror and realistically describe what you see) and the metaphorical one (you look at yourself in other people's eyes; sociology calls it a "social mirror").[Frank, M. G., and Ekman, P., 1993; Schneider, K., and Josephs, I., 1991; Gunnery, S. D., and Hall, J. A.; 2014]

Day	Emotion felt	Body appearance (in your own eyes)	Body appearance (in the eyes of others)

Based on the information obtained, make a "joy list" - a list of people, places, things, and things that make you happy, make you smile, put a twinkle in your eye, and make you feel great. Hang it in a visible place - above the bed or on the fridge. Look at it several times a day and adjust events in such a way (go to certain places, meet the right people, etc.) so that you have reasons to be happy as often as possible.

Think positive!

Negativity and nihilism are weapons that kill. If you always say "no" and keep repeating that it won't work, you condemn yourself to a sad and miserable life in which there is no room for joy, love, enthusiasm, or hope. Gloominess, constant pessimism, and a skeptical attitude result in the growth of negative emotions and, consequently, self-destruction. The negativity of thoughts and beliefs creates an attitude full of doubt and a lack of trust toward others. Even in the face of positive events and a successful turn of events, a person disbelieves, doubts, questions, deprecates, and denies. The future fills him with great fear, which further strengthens his catastrophic thinking.

Rejecting pessimism cultivates positive thinking. Train yourself to create positive thoughts, and use every opportunity to do so - a queue at a doctor's office, riding a tram, waiting for a late bus. Remember that positivity breeds happiness, while negativity takes it away, making us bitter, territorial, and closed to the charms of everyday life. An emotionally intelligent person tries to think positively because he knows that positivity allows us to flourish. What is this flourishing? As Barbara L. Fredrickson points out, flourishing is not only about life satisfaction and happiness but also about giving goodness and joy to others, making the world a better place by getting involved in your family and community, in your work, and your hobbies. Flourishing people have a set agenda and function with a sense of purpose. Flourishing is doing valuable things every day.

It involves crossing the boundaries of selfishness and sharing what is good and beautiful with others.[Fredrickson BL, 1998]

Social isolation, interpersonal hermeticity, and closedness associated with aversion to others may be caused, on the one hand, by shyness or fear of something new and unknown, and thus perceived as dangerous and threatening, and on the other hand, result from a supernatural sense of shame and a constantly felt humiliation. These feelings become a feature of people who cannot accept themselves because they often become objects of ridicule, humiliation, public ridicule, or ridicule. Weakened self-esteem means that many events (devoid of any subtext or meaning) are perceived as directly aimed at these people, intended to hurt or insult. Wanting to avoid further humiliation, such people shift the blame onto those around them and accuse them of acting to the detriment of others.

Try this!

Try to abandon your standard beliefs and opinions for at least a few days (especially if you are fixated on a certain idea, political option, or worldview). Consider that you may be wrong or only partially right and that what someone else says is also valid. In short – open yourself to otherness (other people, other tastes, other visions of the world and lifestyles)! Look at people, trying to accept as fully as possible what they say, eat, wear, what they look like, and how they behave. Don't comment, don't judge, don't criticize. Just absorb their differentness. Then write down what the experience taught you (showed).

Conclusions from observations: ....
....
....
....
....

Both positive and negative emotions are a simple consequence of interpreting certain events, and assessing them from a certain angle, from a subjective perspective. An identical event may be perceived as positive by one person and a failure by another. This method of interpretation translates directly into the activity undertaken and the approach to the problem by making various attempts to solve it. People who think positively and thus focus on the advantages in interpreting events (emphasizing the pluses instead of the minuses) tolerate failures and cope with loss better. Remember: there are various losses in life - money, honor, respect, a loved one, health. However, some losses may turn out to be gains.

The Pollyanna effect is positive thinking and only considering the bright sides of life. Pollyanna (the title character of Eleanor H. Porter's novel) could be happy even in difficult times, and she always had a radiant smile on her face.[Dember, W. N., & Penwell, L., 1980; Goodhart, D. E., 1985;Zheng, X., Wu, B., Li, C. S., Zhang, P., & Tang, N., 2021]

7 - PRACTICAL EMOTIONAL INTELLIGENCE. IMPORTANT INFORMATION

You need to do this

You've come a long way in working through your emotions. It certainly took a lot of effort and effort, but you know it was worth it. The changes that occurred at the behavioral, cognitive, and biophysical levels made your life better. Remember to never stop working on your emotional intelligence, because its level can always be higher, and thus you can live better and smarter. To expand the boundaries of IE and improve the acquired competencies, make (from memory) a summary list that will include a list of the skills included in IE. Place a (+), (+/–), or (–) sign next to each of the competencies listed, depending on how you assess its mastery and implementation. Then complete the sentences below the list.

Take into account skills such as empathy, self-control, positive thinking, accepting flaws and weaknesses, forgiving mistakes, liking yourself, respect for the body, proper self-esteem, conscientiousness, openness to others, the ability to cooperate, effective communication, and understanding.

....

› Skills fully mastered (+): ....

....

....
› What does it say about me that I have fully mastered these skills?

....

....

› Skills mastered approximately (+/−): ....

....

....

› What does it say about me that I have half or some mastery of these skills?

....

....

› Skills not mastered at all (−): ....

....

....

› What does the lack of these skills say about me?

Improving emotional intelligence involves building and accumulating resources (acquiring new skills and consolidating those already acquired), which, using economic metaphors, can be compared to stocking up for the winter. Foresighted farmers and resourceful housewives know that every year comes a dead period when the land does not produce crops. Similarly, there are infertile moments in life when we lack internal nourishment and feel completely barren - this is when we should reach for previously accumulated reserves, which in scientific language are referred to as social resources. Building resources, like stockpiling, requires hard work, effort, and commitment, but it pays off tremendously in the long run. When we have something to draw from, we can survive moments of crisis and emerge unscathed from the greatest difficulties. So start stocking up in advance - winter comes to everyone.

You need to have a good impression of yourself!
Many people have a low opinion of themselves and low self-esteem, which causes many difficulties in their personal and professional lives and prevents full personality development. The reasons for this should be found in childhood and the lack of full

acceptance from parents or guardians. If you think negatively and critically about yourself, other people think the same about you, because, on a subconscious level, you are sending them such information about yourself. Change it! Ask a few people from your close environment (friends, acquaintances, siblings) to write on a piece of paper what they think about you, what they value about you, and what they like, charm, and delight about you. How do you impress them, why are you important and helpful to them? Collect the cards and, based on the assessments contained on them, build an in-depth image of yourself, without any comments from the author. See how well people think of you, how happy they are that you are with them!

Others about me – summary:

....
....
....
....
....
....

Time to love yourself

Some people think that self-love is bad because it shows selfishness, autoeroticism, and narcissistic preoccupation. Nothing could be further from the truth. Love for Self is the condition for giving this feeling to others - in accordance with the commandment "Love your neighbor as yourself." So if you don't love yourself, you are incapable of loving anyone. Loving yourself means standing in the truth - being authentic regardless of the situation, not simulating emotions, not playing the game of appearances, not manipulating impressions, not proving anything to anyone. Stop pretending to be someone you're not. Artificiality and theatricality are based on falsehood, which is always recognizable and discouraging. Be honest with yourself and others, let your thoughts, words, and actions be one. Then you will feel peace and harmony, internal splits will disappear, and you will gain a sense of reconciliation with yourself. Loving yourself means respecting your own achievements, experiences, and experiences.

Your entire life story makes up who and what you are. As you analyze your life, understand that your story is unique. Through this, realize that you are unique and one of a kind. Be amazed by yourself – body and mind. Admire what you value in yourself, but also what you did not want to accept from fate, but became yours. If something bothers you – change it; and if you cannot change something, accept it with approval.

Exercise

Designate a specific time during the day (e.g. 5:15 p.m.) when you will slander yourself - think and talk about yourself falsely and brutally, and throw slander, insults, and curses at yourself. Scream at yourself, don't spare insults. Be ruthless, rude, and vulgar. Point out everything, every mistake, the slightest offense. And so on for a month, always at the same time.

This exercise is provocative - after a month you will notice that you no longer want to think and talk badly about yourself, and the words you used to accuse, blame, and slander yourself will now seem grotesque and ridiculous.

To love yourself is to accept yourself fully, without any "buts". Accept yourself as you are, with all your flaws, weaknesses, limitations, deeply hidden stupidity, poverty, and hopelessness. Not only successes and moments of triumph make life - failures, doubts, and dramas are also a part of it. Accept that you don't know something, that you can't do something, that you stutter, turn red and sweat, that you have protruding ears, sparse hair, cellulite, that you haven't been somewhere, that you didn't do something even though you should have, or that you did something even though you shouldn't. Don't beat yourself up about it and don't blame yourself - the past can't be changed, and by condemning yourself, you're standing still or taking a step back instead of taking a step forward. Be yourself, live your life - some people waste a lot of time and energy on pretending and creating characters they would like to be. Let go of illusions and illusions. People carry false ideas, obligations, and expectations in their heads about what they should be like. If we took a closer look at these demands, it would turn out that they were the voice of a parent who said what should and should not be allowed. Tear off the mask and show others your true face. Don't be afraid that this will make you lose value or sympathy from others, that you will become an object of ridicule or pity, or that they will reject you or not accept you into their close circle. This may happen, but the feeling of comfort and relief that exposure will bring will set you free. Don't worry about what others will think and say about you, or how they will react when they see the truth about you. Allow yourself to feel what you want to feel, say what you want to say, think the way you want to think, and do what you think is good for you. Release blocked layers of emotions, both positive and negative. Experience these emotions: when you feel joy, laugh out loud; when you feel sad, cry. If you suppress these emotions and accumulate them inside yourself, you destroy yourself from the inside, which makes you look at yourself even more hatefully. Many people block emotions at their own request; they probably once decided that it's better not to feel anything - it makes life easier and hurts less. Indifference became for them a life insurance policy without tears and suffering that penetrates the marrow of the bones. To neutralize is to freeze emotions so that they do not produce their natural effects. In fact, in some situations, the lack of feeling brings relief, but at the same time, it numbs you to the most beautiful experiences that are worth experiencing, even if they last for a short time. Let yourself melt just a little. If you access your emotions and open yourself to them, you will gain new strength and feel life. There are many different ways to access emotions, such as laughter, singing, dancing, prayer, yoga, and breathing exercises.

Exercise
The body dances and the soul sings
Dress to please yourself, put on your favorite tune, and start dancing. Sing, smile, just listen to the music. Dance the way you like, don't worry about making mistakes, not moving to the rhythm, or looking funny. Just dance! Do this exercise several times a week for at least a month. After each dance session, write down what you feel (name your emotions as precisely as possible).

Live in harmony with yourself

People often underestimate what they have, always wanting more and more, or wanting something completely different. Even if they achieve a lot and get to where they previously planned - where they feel the best, they devote all their energy to matters that in hindsight do not make much sense, they miss the most beautiful moments, and life slips through their fingers. Each of us deals with many things in life, meets many people, is interested in various matters, and is stuck in a cycle of tasks and responsibilities. However, in all this, you should learn to separate the most important matters from those that are less important or those that are completely meaningless. Give attention and time to people, not things, work to live - not live to work.

Exercise
Set your priorities
Make a list of 10 people, things, issues, or events that are important to you. Next to it, write down how much time you devote to them (in hours per day). After completing the table, write down who/what you spend the most time on and whether it is a good investment for the future.

Persons	Things	Events

Am I investing my time well? If not, how could I improve my time management?

....
....
....

Only a free person can be happy, and he can only lead a life in harmony with himself. So do what you like, surround yourself with people you love, and stay in places where you feel good and safe. Let everything in your life be the result of free choice, not top-down coercion. If you remain free, you will achieve the desired state of inner peace and harmony in which you will be able to enjoy every moment and appreciate the taste of life.

There is also a large group of people who have been generously gifted by fate - it has given them health, long life, wonderful children, true friends, many kind people on their path, attractive jobs, etc. Despite this, they do not appreciate their wealth. Moreover, they constantly complain, criticize, or lament about their "misfortune." Maybe they are playing with fate? They usually begin to realize how much they have when they lose everything (they become seriously ill, their child dies, and they are left with no means of subsistence). Don't allow yourself to appreciate the amount of happiness you have in your life only in the face of loss.

List in a table the people, things, and situations you always or often complain about. Next to it, write how you would feel if you lost them all irrevocably.

Who or what am I complaining about?	How would I feel if I lost it?

Do not judge

Judging has become a part of our blood. We have been accustomed to it from the beginning of our lives: first, the assessment on the Apgar point scale, then, over the long years of education, school grades, ranging from unsatisfactory to excellent, was a formalized tool for informing about our knowledge, talent, and skills. We are so used to giving grades that it is difficult for some people to imagine that they could not be subject to grades, and also not judge anyone or pass judgments themselves. Many people cannot stop themselves from censoring people. This is especially done by those who cannot tolerate ambiguity and uncertainty. People or situations that are not fully defined defy simplified classification and can very easily be judged harshly, especially by those who cannot accept interpersonal differences and operate under the assumption that everyone should be similar to them in terms of mentality, worldview, and even physical (if someone dresses or does their hair differently, has a different skin color or eye shape, they are perceived as worse and stupider). Strict judges are so eager and quick to judge primarily because they don't think the best of themselves, but instead of admitting it and starting to change, they suppress emotions related to low self-esteem. By judging others, they remove their internal feeling of inferiority or inferiority, putting themselves in the position of someone free from flaws or imperfections. At the same time, people who judge so often, and even claim the right to do so, are very afraid of judgments themselves - when they are judged negatively or even less positively than they would like, they react with aggression and anger.

Assessments can be filled with various emotional content. As a rule, they are related to the mood at a given moment: if we are happy, the assessments are flattering and understanding, but if we carry a lot of anger within us, the assessments are radically lower and unfair. The assessment mechanism is activated in almost all everyday situations: during social conversations, family meetings, going to church, at the cinema, or the restaurant. We assess to minimize the possible cognitive effort necessary to maintain a sense of ontological security, i.e. awareness of who a given person is and what should be expected from him. Therefore, using even a cursory assessment of external appearance - e.g. "She is pretty" - we generalize about the individual, attributing to him several other features, such as honesty, intelligence, and personal culture.

Fun fact

The halo effect is the tendency to evaluate and describe people according to the favorable or unfavorable impression they have made on us. For example, we glorify physically attractive people, assigning them - based on their appearance - several secondary traits, such as intelligence, cordiality, openness, and kindness.

Assessments are not a fully reliable medium of information about anyone or anything, primarily because in the assessment process we make many cognitive errors and fall into thinking traps. Sometimes, at first glance, we think we know what behavior is good and right, what is bad and condemnable, who deserves recognition, and who should be stigmatized. We evaluate according to arbitrary criteria - those that, based on the social contract, we consider appropriate and fit the coded image of the world. As a rule, certain behaviors have a clear classification (e.g. murder is a reprehensible and punishable act), but many other behaviors are relative, which means that their assessment depends on several personality and situational conditions. Often, when looking for the reasons for some behavior, instead of taking into account the situation in which the individual finds himself, we point to his character traits, including dispositions, attributes, and capabilities. We thus commit the fundamental attribution error.

Fun fact

The fundamental attribution error is the tendency to attribute too much importance to personality factors compared to environmental and situational factors. In an ambiguous situation, people tend to judge according to their beliefs and prejudices. For example: if Mr. X sees an elegantly dressed white man sitting on a park bench in the afternoon, the sight does not evoke any pejorative associations. If the man was black, then Mr X would have believed that he was dealing with a good-for-nothing and a slacker who lives off his taxes.

When assessing the situation you find yourself in, the people who stand in your way, the events that you accept or not, but nevertheless happen to you, remember to be prudential, moderate, calm and conservative. Don't judge hastily, hold off on your judgment, both harsh and inflated, as long as possible. Give yourself time, postpone the moment when you say with full confidence that someone is this way and not that way, when you put a label on someone that is difficult to remove. Of course, some degree of evaluation is needed, primarily to differentiate the value of people and things, to know what to expect from someone and when, thus avoiding further misunderstandings or unpleasant situations. However, you should exercise restraint in your assessments, especially when it comes to situations when you draw conclusions about people around you based on weak and unconfirmed premises. Know that the way you judge the behavior of others most often results from who you are and what the motives are for your behavior - according to the principle "Everyone judges for themselves."

Exercise

Don't judge, just watch

Go to a crowded place – a train station, a movie theater, a popular restaurant, a hypermarket – and look at the people you meet. Mentally describe and characterize them, but avoid judgment. For example, say that the lady at the checkout is wearing a pink blouse, but reject the urge to judge whether the blouse is tasteful or tacky, whether the woman looks good in it or not. After performing the experiment, write down what, in your opinion, is the difference between an evaluative look and a concluding look (stating facts).

Now write down your own conclusions:

....

....

8 – YOUR EMOTIONAL INTELLIGENT LOVER

Anyone who creates a successful relationship knows that it is not easy. It's not enough to just love, you also have to make every effort to make the relationship develop and flourish. Just like a gardener who plants a rose must take care of it – water and fertilize it; otherwise, the plant will wither or go wild. Remember: it is not enough to create a relationship and sanction it in the registry office. Much more is needed - above all, respect, care, patience, attention, and commitment. A relationship is about being together, that is, being interested in your partner (what he thinks and feels, how he evaluates and values), actively participating in his life, accompanying him, and looking in one direction. There can be no destructive emotions in love, such as hatred, aggression, anger, morbid jealousy, the will to take revenge, regret, etc. All it takes is for one of them to appear and - regardless of its intensity - the relationship begins to wither. If you do not try to save it then, it will soon cease to exist. In love, you must be vigilant, like a guard on guard, answering questions every day about what your relationship looks like now, what condition it is in, what you did today to improve it, and what behavior was inappropriate or hurtful.

Of course, most of us realize that love must be strived for and cultivated. However, how to get involved if your partner completely disregards you, how to trust her/him if she/he cheats, how to love her/him when you become indifferent to her/him, how to maintain passion when work and excessive responsibilities are stressful? It's very difficult because you start to get carried away with honor or you give up, saying that it's not worth it anymore, that there's no point. Meanwhile, you are afraid to dig deep and find the cause of the problems. You are afraid to admit that the fault is also on your side.

You have to do this!
Write down everything that bothers you in your relationship, what bothers you and irritates you (e.g. your partner's faults, habits, behavior). Then, use the sideways arrow technique (analogous to the example) to try to discover the source of the problem.

My wife/husband sits in a chair all day after work. → she/he says he is tired. → she/he takes over time. → I want to earn more money → We are planning a holiday by the sea. → Sacrifices for the family.

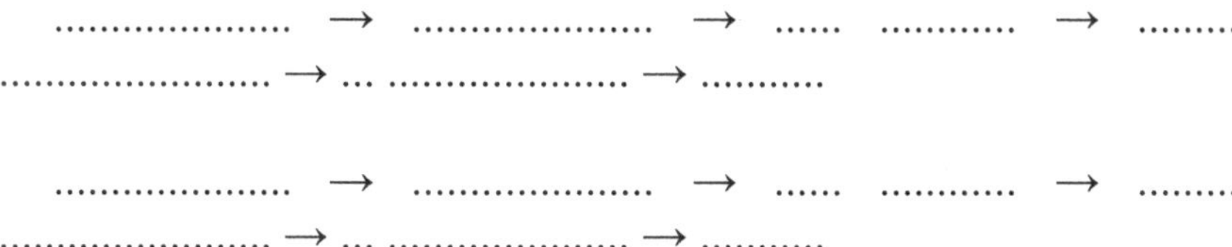

When deciding to be with someone, you should know what you expect from your partner and what you are unable to accept. This knowledge is the foundation of a good relationship, but building subsequent levels requires not only formulating expectations but also meeting them. You are making a big mistake by looking for fulfillment outside yourself and counting on your partner to make you happy, compensate for the losses incurred so far, and settle the accounts of wrongs suffered. If you want to build a happy relationship, you should first find the values you expect from a partner, and fully accept and love yourself. Only then will you be able to give love to others and notice and accept another person's love.

Usually, every relationship, and certainly the vast majority of them, starts similarly - with falling in love. Falling in love is a specific mental and emotional state. Numerous biochemical processes take place in the body, hormones are raging, blood circulates faster, and a person lives in the ecstasy of love. This condition is exhausting for the body, but - as those who have experienced it know - also fantastic and unique. During the period of falling in love, the partner seems to be a walking ideal, without the slightest flaw. Over time, however, the elation wears off and the rose-colored glasses through which we looked at the relationship fall off. If falling in love is not a result of true and deep love, partners begin to quarrel, cheat, and even hate each other. Relationships fail, people break up, or worse, they stay stuck in this unhealthy situation, languishing and bitter.

So it's time to look at the relationship from a different perspective. When he or she does not meet your expectations, when you feel disappointed by your partner's actions, or when you lack satisfaction and happiness, you should develop emotional intelligence. Start by carefully observing your behavior - analyze what you think and say about your partner and your relationship, and what actions result from these thoughts and words. Listen to how you address your partner - what words you use, what tone you use, and whether you open up space when your partner speaks. Think about how you look at her/him (or do you look at all?). Pay attention to how your words and actions affect your partner, what actions make him happy, and what makes her/him sad.

Keep it in your mind!

The essence of emotional intelligence is understanding that the quality and durability of your relationship depend on you. Love, trust, and joy come from you and you get in return exactly what you give. If you have never been able to offer another person affection, care, attention, and respect - don't expect it in return. Your relationship can only be successful if you give your all, work on yourself, make an effort to give your partner happiness, convey joy and optimism, and support and comfort him when needed.

Of course, some relationships are so damaged that there is no point in saving them. Then the partners should show responsibility and decide to break up. There is nothing worse than staying in a toxic relationship against your or your partner's will, poisoning your life and the lives of others. An emotionally mature person can walk away from everything that does not strengthen him, develop him, or make him happy. Of course, there are people who, regardless of the damage incurred and caused, remain in toxic relationships, cannot leave each other, and are addicted to the pain and suffering they cause to each other. They are emotional masochists. They like the situation they find themselves in, their behavior forces violence and humiliation on their partner, and they provoke them to suffer a mental or physical blow. Paradoxically: the situation when they suffer satisfies them, a sense of security and self-confidence. They strive to assume the role of victim because being unhappy, tormented, and sad is a source of pleasure and fulfillment for them.

Important

In criminology, the term "Stockholm syndrome" was coined to describe the phenomenon when a victim sympathizes with a perpetrator of violence. Despite the harm and pain suffered, as well as numerous acts of aggression by the attacker, the victim is attached to him and feels relieved when he is next to him.

When deciding to be with someone, be aware that you should accept the other person with all the benefits of the inventory: flaws, shortcomings, weaknesses, irritating manner, annoying habits, and old habits. Entering a relationship means deciding that you want to be with a given person, you accept them and accept them as they are. If it doesn't suit you and you can't accept something about it, then don't enter into this relationship. If you hope that your partner will change after the wedding and adapt to your requirements, that you will mold her/him in your way, you are making a mistake. The only thing you can change in your relationship is yourself, your behavior, and your approach to the other person. No one has a magic wand that can transform their partner into their dream Princess/Prince Charming, but we can change ourselves and it is thanks to this change that we can influence the rest.

If you constantly live in a world of delusion, you keep repeating that you "imagined it differently", that "the world turned out not to be what you thought", that "you wanted to live differently" - it's time to shake off your childish and fairy-tale visions. Creating illusions is typical of children or emotionally immature adults who cannot realize their dreams through their own activity, so they conjure reality to adapt to their expectations. Remember: if you want to make your life better, make your dreams come true, and achieve a certain level of perfection, you must put in huge physical and mental effort, combined with sacrifice, a sense of discomfort, fatigue, and inconvenience. Figuratively speaking, it takes sweat, blood and tears. Achieving goals and aspirations, reaching peaks, and improving yourself is a murderous path. If you walk it patiently, despite many difficult passages and sharp turns, while maintaining healthy self-discipline - be sure that you will be able to live the life you dreamed of. And if you stray from this path or don't make an effort to follow it at all, don't blame anyone that your life is different than you wanted.

An emotionally intelligent person realizes that life is full of light and shadow, joy, and sadness, so you have to take it as it is. So don't fill your mind with ideas about what would happen if... Return to reality, live the life you have, and if you want to change it, then - instead of getting irritated, complaining, whining - take a specific activity, take at least a small step forward.

Say what you feel

The role of interpersonal communication in social life cannot be overestimated. It is communication that makes us social beings - thanks to the fact that we can speak, and therefore convey certain content to others, receive and process it, we are able to get to know the surrounding reality, explain the phenomena occurring in it, and understand the people around us. Communication (Latin: communio) means community, connection, connection. The etymology of the word well reflects the main meaning of communication, which is establishing relationships, being together, establishing a community, and maintaining closeness. Social relationships and networks can be shaped through regular, efficient, and in-depth communication. Communication allows you to meet another person, and exchange thoughts and feelings. In the process of building a relationship, this is of fundamental importance because only those who are in direct contact are close.

Cordial, open, and at the same time factual communication is the basis of a successful relationship. For the communication process to proceed correctly and effectively, two conditions should be met: firstly, you should speak clearly and unpretentiously; second, you need to listen (and not just hear) what your partner is saying. Regardless of what thoughts and feelings you have, communicate them in an unrestrained and unambiguous way (of course, not everyone and not always should talk about your deepest feelings - emotional exhibitionism can only appear when you are close to each other, in an atmosphere of complete trust and understanding). By opening up to your partner, you will feel the depth and truthfulness of your relationship. Conversation, and not just a casual exchange of sentences, involves presenting each other's needs and desires, pointing out important things, setting priorities, and clarifying misunderstandings. The conversation should be authentic - don't hide anything, play your cards open, and reveal your emotions and beliefs. If you manage to have a real conversation, you will enter a space where your visions of the world begin to interpenetrate and complement each other. Then you will be really close.

The condition for agreement and understanding is empathy, which is based on the assumption that to experience the world with another person and notice their feelings and needs, we must reject prejudices and stereotypes. When talking to your partner, adopt an empathetic attitude, and let go of the belief that you know what he means, what he wants to say, and what the truth is. Don't finish speaking for him, don't suggest anything. Just listen to what he says with interest, understanding, warmth, and openness. Receive his story as if he were telling you about the most important thing in life, and direct yourself to understand it. Even if he talks about extremely boring and banal matters, don't ignore his words, don't say: "We'll talk tomorrow", "I don't have time", or "Talk to your friends". It is conversations and confessions that cement your relationship, making it unique, one of a kind - that's why the more you talk, the more harmonious a duo you become. When listening to your partner's story, carefully follow every aspect of the statement, concentrate on the words being spoken, and on body language to also catch unspoken messages. Don't interrupt, don't comment, don't judge, don't impose your point of view, don't give advice (unless he specifically asks for it), don't put questions in the crossfire. A conversation is primarily about meeting two people, mutual understanding, and honest expression of what one feels and thinks. If you adopt a judgmental or radicalized attitude, true unification will never occur. When your partner finishes speaking, try to let him know that you understood exactly what he said.

Scientific research shows that the main causes of breakups or divorces are four negative interactions (symbolically called the "four horsemen of the apocalypse"): complaint/criticism, contempt, building a wall, and defensive attitude. A complaint arises from a difference of opinion or anger that morphs into judgmental and blaming criticism. Contempt is insulting, mocking, ridiculing, or ironizing; it is intended to discredit the other person and humiliate him. Building a wall involves disregarding the person speaking, which is expressed by a lack of reaction to his words - the result is a barrier and lack of understanding. Emotionally, the speaker perceives the listener as cold, indifferent, calculating, and even hostile. However, a defensive posture is adopted to protect oneself from an attack or to repel it. Manifestations of such an attitude include, among others: counter-attacking and shifting responsibility.

How to face the four dark and evil horsemen?

Dark and evil horsemen	How to defeat him?
Accusation/criticism	
Contempt/scorn/disdain	
The invisible crushing wall	
Defensive stance	

It is very possible you already dealt with these dark and evil horsemen in your life.

Be understanding towards your partner. Avoid personal accusations and grievances such as: "You wasted my life", "Because of you I am unhappy", "If it weren't for you, I would have achieved more", "You are a loser/laissez-faire/idiot", "You always.../you never... ". It is a language of hatred that causes negative reactions - the partner will respond even more severely or feel deeply hurt. Perhaps even to the point of questioning the meaning and future of your relationship. Words are like thrown stones - they have deadly power and even if you don't think what you said, everything you say stays in your memory for a long time. Some words are hard to forget and forgive. So control what you say. An intelligent person realizes the great power of words, which is why he always knows what he says, and does not - he says what he knows.

This is a must-do!

The school of silence

Silence is an extremely difficult art. While most people acquired the ability to speak in early childhood (around the age of three), not everyone learned to remain silent. It is not without reason that in many cloistered orders, the principle of lex silenti - the law of silence - applies. Silence is conducive to thinking, reflection, and in-depth reflection. If you want to improve your relationship, be silent for a moment. Be there, a companion, but don't say anything, and express what you want to say with a look, a touch, a gesture. Think about yourself: why do you want so much to have the last word, to stand your ground, to convince others that you are right? Are you so unsure of your own beliefs or do you have authoritarian tendencies? Resolve that today you will refrain from unnecessary comments and judgments. Count to 10 before uttering any criticism. If you do point out someone's faults, make sure you say it kindly; criticism should be constructive, otherwise, give up on it. Whenever you feel the need to criticize someone or something, think about why you are so offended by someone's mistakes, mistakes, and decisions. Does that mean you have no flaws? Or do you consider yourself to be someone better, someone who has the right to punish, stigmatize, and set the rules that govern the world? Or maybe you think that it is a sacred duty to show the "only correct" path, to convert those who are mistaken? If you think so, know that it is wrong thinking and the sooner you understand it, the sooner you will become smarter. First, realize that you are who you are, not who you want to think you are. You can only decide about your own fate, so don't interfere in the lives of others, let them live their own way. No matter what you think of others, no matter how much their presence or behavior annoys you or throws you off balance, try to suppress your own irritability. A person's character is exposed by what irritates her/him and causes anger and irritation. Secondly, remember that most of the flaws that you see and stigmatize in others are actually your own flaws - the projection mechanism works here: to free yourself from the flaws that you carry within yourself, you attribute them to other people.

Exercise

My fault

Admitting guilt is the preliminary stage of any change. Admit your mistakes and you will feel lighter and better. Since you may not be aware of some of them, the following exercise will help you learn and acknowledge your flaws. Think about what annoys you in other people, what features you cannot tolerate, what irritates you. Name each feature, then try to define it (what is it, when does it occur, what does it mean?), then reverse the pattern and recognize (perhaps initially you will resist) that it is your flaw. Say it out loud, acknowledge its existence.

What annoys her/him?	What is the trait?	I confess I am…
1. Untidiness 2. 3.	1. scattered clothes, dirty windows, unwashed dishes 2. 3.	1. Messy 2. 3.

Look at the relationship through your lover's eyes

It often happens that people who enter into a relationship are completely unaware of what life as a couple is like. The only information about happy marriages comes from romantic movies or Harlequin movies with cheesy happy endings. They imagine that it all begins with first sight and a passionate kiss, and then they live happily ever after. But what to do in a situation that resembles a scene from a horror movie rather than a fairy tale - when the princess turns back into a toad and the prince on a white horse loses his princely manners or his kisses no longer come to life? Confronting reality can then hurt. Know that real life is different from a fairy tale. Unrealistic thinking based on utopian visions makes us feel disappointed and embittered as the relationship continues because it differs significantly from the images of love presented in romance novels. Of course, this does not mean that romanticism is unnecessary in a relationship and should be given up. However, as you know from the previous chapters of the book, a balance between heart and mind is necessary.

Emotional intelligence in a relationship is knowledge about how this relationship functions, what principles it is based on, and what are the weaknesses of your relationship. In other words: what is missing in your relationship? Together with your partner, try to answer this question comprehensively, using the "seeing through the eyes of the other" technique. Each of you should answer the following questions as precisely as possible from your partner's perspective - as if you were in his/her place and were his/her porte-parole. Imagine her/him sitting in front of you and patiently answering the following questions:

› What could I do for you to make you feel better in our relationship?

....
....

› What makes you happy, gives you joy and pleasure?

....
....

› What good words would you like to hear from me?

....
....

› What behaviors, gestures, and looks of mine do you like the most?

....
....

› What moment of our life together do you remember most fondly? When were you the happiest?

....
....

› What moment of our lives do you remember the worst? When were you unhappy?

....

Once you have finished filling in the boxes, read the answers aloud. This is a good moment to confront each other's ideas about the relationship. Compare the answers - where they overlap and where they diverge. Discuss why you disagreed and why you thought differently.

Make your partner happy

To make someone happy means to make them feel good, light, nice, at ease, and wonderful. Happiness is the best gift you can give to another person, and – importantly – it pays off quickly. According to the principle of the gift economy, you will receive what you give. So if you give happiness, it will come back to you, making you feel great too. In short, by making others happy, you make yourself happy. So learn to bring happiness to those around you.

Exercise

In the emotion organizer, draw a four-column table. Decide that you will give something to your partner every day for a week. It's not so much about material things but about spiritual and symbolic things (a kind word, a compliment, a smile, attention, help, closeness). In the following columns, write down what your gift was, how your partner reacted, and what you felt then.

Day	What did you give	Lover's reaction	What did you feel?
Sunday			
Monday			
Tuesday			
Wednesday			
Thursday			
Friday			
Saturday			

After this exercise, summarize and draw conclusions. Circle the gift that you think made your partner the happiest. Why do you think this one? What need of his have you met at this point? What did you give him through your gift? If you answered these questions, you probably already know what makes your partner happy, and what words or gestures bring about his joy, humor, and well-being. Go in this direction.

A relationship can only be happy when it is created by happy people, i.e. those who are satisfied with their lives, derive satisfaction from what they do and who they are, and emanate warmth, goodness, and kindness. If you have negative emotions such as jealousy, envy, anger, etc., you will never be happy and therefore you will not bring happiness to others. Happiness is not given in advance, it does not come from outside, from outside us. It requires building or finding it within yourself, sometimes appreciating how much you have and how lucky you are. Maybe your relationship isn't bringing you joy, something is missing in it, or something is bothering you. You can change this by enriching your story with new elements. Below is the pentalogue of happiness, a set of five commandments that must be followed to build a great relationship.

1. First commandment: show gratitude

Gratitude is the joy of receiving a gift, the awareness of experiencing a benefit. To create a sense of gratitude, analyze every day how many good things you received from your partner today (e.g. a tasty dinner, an unusual compliment, a tender look, an ironed shirt, and earrings as a gift). Appreciate everything that has happened to you and thank you with a word or gesture. A great sin is ingratitude, treating gifts as debts, and overlooking the unique nature of the people, situations, and events we encounter. Be grateful for today and express that gratitude because you may miss tomorrow. The more gratitude you have, your partner will feel appreciated and confident of your devotion and love.

2. Second commandment: be optimistic

Another condition for a happy relationship is optimism. Of course, this is not about hurray-optimism, detachment from the earth, and high-in-the-clouds. We are talking about a fact-based and rationalized attempt to look at events and the existing situation in a positive way, filled with hope and faith that even if today is bad, tomorrow can be better. There are moments when it is difficult to find even the slightest sign of optimism. Then it is most difficult to discover and resurrect it in yourself. To think optimistically, you must remember that the meaning of life is change, things will never be the same, and you cannot keep both happiness and unhappiness for long. This belief will allow you to believe that all bad things will end sooner or later, that sadness does not last forever, and that sunshine always comes out after the storm. Life is easier for optimists because they do not torment themselves with bad feelings, they live in the hope that things will work out, and they see the glass half full. Therefore, they do not provoke misfortunes. Positive thinking is extremely important because, according to the principle of self-fulfilling prophecy, if you think something will happen to you (both positive and negative), it will happen.

So if you want life to go your way, be an optimist and spread that optimism. When you notice that your partner is worried or sees everything bleak, show her the other (brighter) side of the situation. For example, if she lost her job, remind her that now she has a chance to rest and improve her qualifications, and then find another one, better paid and more satisfying.

3. Third Commandment: DON'T COMPARE YOURSELF OR YOUR PARTNER TO ANYONE!

Never describe either yourself or your partner through comparisons, either to those who are worse or better than you. If you compare yourself with inferiors (downward social comparison), you become proud, brash, arrogant, and haughty. This, in turn, strengthens a false sense of advantage over other people. In this way, you adopt an egocentric attitude, which breeds egoism - the cause of many human misfortunes. However, if you compare yourself with those who are better (upward social comparison), you become resentful, resentful, and insecure, and you become convinced that you cannot meet life's challenges and that you are of little consequence. So: avoid comparisons, be your own authority, and treat yourself as a separate frame of reference. Don't think about what others will say, act in harmony with yourself, that is, so that you don't feel cognitive dissonance when making a choice. Remember that every comparison starts a whole chain of distorted beliefs and can negatively affect your social relationships, reducing their quality and quantity. A person who constantly compares himself cannot develop a true identity -

instead, he constructs a false self-image based on comparative fixations.

4.   Fourth commandment: feel joy

You would like to remain in joy forever because then you feel happy and fulfilled. It is a state of elation and delight and at the same time bliss and peace. When you feel joy, you laugh, open up to people, and enjoy life, which makes it easier to free yourself from anxiety, sadness, and anger. Buddhists claim that joy is a natural emotional state and occurs when a person goes beyond his own limitations, defeats demons, and crosses the limits of anxiety, fear, hysteria, and gloominess. By breaking down internal barriers, you achieve a state of mind when you are fully reconciled with fate, with others, and with yourself. Then you touch the part of yourself that is the most true, in which you feel fully yourself, you completely accept yourself, and you feel good about yourself. Joy comes from kindness, affirmation, and self-distance. You experience it in various situations, sometimes, paradoxically, not very joyful or even painful, cruel, devoid of the recommended subtlety and elegance. No matter how bad your situation is, find joy within yourself and share it with your partner. Give him love, goodness, cheerfulness, and a smile; support you in pursuing your goal and realizing your dreams; make him feel great; bring pleasures and pleasant surprises. Enjoy your partner - the fact that you see him, that you are with him, that you talk together, eat a meal, rest, and make love. Think and speak well of him. Treat it as a miracle that happens only once in your life.

5. The fifth commandment: forgive

There is no perfect relationship. Now and then, things get worse: grudges and reproaches appear, arguments break out, misunderstandings occur, and "quiet days" come. Accept it as the natural order of things, an indispensable attribute of being together. Remember, however, never to hold a grudge, but to forgive, reject anger, and forgive transgressions. Respond to apologies and expressions of regret, instead of getting offended, sulking, bragging, and feeling misguided pride. This is very discouraging from trying to re-explain the situation. If you cannot forgive, you build a barrier that begins to build resentment, hostility, and even the will to take revenge. Of course, some things are particularly difficult to forgive (betrayal, lies, violence, insults) - the one who can forgive them is a man of great stature, an emotional hero. Know that you are not obliged to forgive the guilt and harm suffered. If you don't want or can't forgive, leave and end the relationship - there is no other solution, because you can't continue to create a community if you feel wronged. However, if you decide to forgive, let your decision be binding. Don't go back to what happened, don't fester, don't scratch, don't make it clear that you're still going through it. Just forgive me! Of course, it's not about erasing something from your memory (you can't do that), it's about continuing to live with the knowledge you have, moving on to the next (higher) level, closing one stage of life to open the next one. In a situation of feeling harmed or unintentionally suffering, there are three ways of reacting. First, you can deny that something has happened to you (but as you know from reading this guide, denial or denial are not good methods of dealing with the problem). Secondly, you can admit that it affected you, but downplay it - saying, for example, "It didn't matter much to me", and "Nothing like that happened" (this is also not a mature mechanism). Thirdly, you can point out the real extent of the pain your partner caused you and work through the resentment - admit that what happened hurt you and touched you deeply, but you decide to move on because you care about the relationship, you feel better when You are together.

Deepen your bond

Connection, from a sociological point of view, is the basis of human relationships. It is a specific sense of closeness based on the belief that we have something in common, that we have something in common. There are different types of bonds - the division is made depending on what the bond results from and what it is based on. If the bond results from feelings (as in the case of a relationship between two people) and the norms and values that are most often associated with these emotions, it is a moral bond. It is a specific type of social bond assuming loyalty, solidarity, and full trust in relation to people included in the "we" category[54].

The basis of the relationship is commitment, i.e. presence, care, support, and being next to each other. Getting involved means living in a relationship, observing it, following what is happening in it, in what direction it is going, and what changes (beneficial and unfavorable) are taking place in it. By doing this, you accompany your partner on a common path, do not lose sight of important events and circumstances, and become sensitive to possible problems that you can nip in the bud. Make sure to ask your partner every day how he feels, what made him sad or happy, how he spent his day, and what he did. However, these questions cannot be intrusive or intrusive. If you see that your partner does not want to speak or responds only in half words, do not pressure, give him time and at the same time show warmth.

The bond comes from closeness or intimacy. The more intimacy is developed, the stronger the bond becomes. Intimate space in a relationship is exclusive and separate, reserved for partners, and available only to them. This concerns both the sexual sphere (your bodies are yours; erotic experiences, moments of rapture and ecstasy, as well as problems or infirmities, remain only for your knowledge) and the mental sphere including shared secrets, shared secrets, thoughts, dreams, and plans.

Discretion, tact, and restraint against physical or mental betrayal of the partner are necessary here. Intimacy requires absolute honesty and trust that you cannot violate. Otherwise, your relationship will be so sterile and worthless that, from a social point of view, it should not exist at all. Remember that trust is an extremely fragile and breakable product, once it is disappointed or even slightly broken, it is difficult to rebuild it. Cultivate trust in your partner - instead of being suspicious, believe that you can rely on him, show this trust. If you see that someone has given you trust, appreciate it, treat this gift with great care, and do everything not to disappoint.

Always keep in mind!

A relationship lives and develops when we are close to each

other, that is, when:

> we talk to each other a lot;

> we trust each other fully;

> we confide in each other, share secrets, gossip harmlessly, make plans;

> we have common passions, interests, and hobbies;

> we integrate by acting together (cooking dinner together, cleaning, renovating);

> we spend time together (watching a movie, walking, shopping);

> we consult, ask for opinions, and ask for advice;

> we have fun together, we have sex;

> we laugh and share energy;

> we report on our day (our stay at work, a professional meeting).

Closeness is a sincere and unforced desire to be with each other. Being together means sharing everything - not only material goods but also non-material goods (time, attention, strength, feelings). Closeness requires thinking in terms of "we, ours", without making clear divisions into "I, you", or "mine, yours". This does not mean the unification of partners, merging into one, losing themselves in themselves. As Anthony Giddens says, "Intimacy is not about merging with the other person, but about getting to know them and opening up to them. Paradoxically, the condition for such openness is the limit of privacy, because it is based on communication and requires sensitivity and tact because it is not about having nothing to hide"[Muniruzzaman, M., 2017]. You should accept that your partner is an individual, and allow him to be himself, instead of changing, modifying, or demanding the total abolition of boundaries. If you try to appropriate your partner and want him to become your property, you lose control and contact with reality. This is how obsession is born: you know the case: you are friendly to X, and from that moment X starts to stalk you.

Remember: lack of trust and violating boundaries will quickly ruin a relationship. To make your relationship thrive, create a space of freedom where your partner feels at ease. Don't limit him by your own fears, bad feelings, moods, low self-esteem, and complexes. Bring fresh air into the relationship, otherwise, you will feel musty and suffocate.

9 - INTELLIGENT EMOTIONAL PARENT

Being a parent is the most serious and responsible job there is. So if you decide to become a parent, be aware that it is a great privilege, but also a challenge that must be met. If you fail and pass the parenting exam, there will be no retake or retake. Therefore, when taking on the role of a mother or father, you must prepare well and know what awaits you and what predispositions this role requires. If you have little or no knowledge, then parenting will overwhelm you and you will be ineffective in this role, harming a defenseless being like your child.

The style and way in which you approach fathering or mothering tasks is largely determined by your life experience - relationships with parents, siblings, and the relationships that prevailed in the family home. If you were constantly emotionally cold and did not feel loved and accepted, it would be difficult for you to revive these emotions and transfer them to your child. The socialization you were subject to during childhood and adolescence shaped your social attitudes, system of norms and values, hierarchies, and priorities. Perhaps you remember your childhood very well - as a period of joy, constant care, and concern. However, it may be that you are reluctant to return to your childhood memories because they bring to mind fear, anxiety, concerns, suffering, and pain. If this is the case, you should go back to your childhood and sort things out from an adult's perspective. Because unless you soothe the hurt child inside you, you cannot be a good parent.

You need to do it!

Take some free time, make sure no one disturbs you, turn off your phone, and don't think about business or shopping. Stay alone with yourself in silence to face your past. Take your childhood album, or if you don't have one, take a photo of yourself from those years. Sit back in your chair and think about the child you see in the photo. Answer the questions:
› What is your first childhood memory? Classify them as positive or negative.
› What great moment from your childhood do you still remember? Who accompanied you then?
› What is your worst memory? Who or what made you feel bad?
› What was the reason you cried the most?
› Is something from your childhood still haunting you (a dream, memory, belief)?

After answering all the questions, diagnose what you felt. You are happy? Or maybe sad and angry? What childhood baggage do you have? If it is particularly heavy, take it off completely or get rid of it at least partially. To do this, stage your childhood, step into the role of a parent, and act it out again - this time based on your script. Imagine a hypothetical situation in which you are your own parent, treat yourself like a child you love more than life, hug, pamper, treat with great delicacy, and constantly show tenderness. Do something for yourself that will make you feel this way - for some, it will be buying a new dress, for others it will be going to an exclusive restaurant, playing bowling, buying a series of books, etc. Don't wonder if it's worth it, if it makes sense, or if it makes sense – just approach yourself as if you were a child whom you want to please. Show yourself tenderness - don't work when you're tired, don't make excuses for not finishing something, failing at a task, or not being perfect. Justify yourself as you would a child. Eat your favorite dish, watch your favorite movie, and make sure you feel great every minute. Now it's time for you to praise your child. Tell yourself loudly and clearly what you always wanted to hear from your parents but were never given, e.g.: "You are beautiful and smart", "I admire you", "I am proud of you", or "You are a precious treasure to me." ", "I love you so much". Perhaps at first repeating this to yourself will seem grotesque and ridiculous, but don't stop, keep repeating it like a mantra. After a few days, you will notice a change - the hurt child who is always crying inside you will find comfort.

Listen to what the child says

A serious mistake made in the educational process is disregarding the child's needs, ignoring what he or she does and says, and treating his or her problems, experiences, and thoughts nonchalantly or frivolously. A child feels and experiences emotions in the same way as an adult, although he expresses and manifests them in his own way. If you have ever questioned your child's feelings by saying, "The problems will only start when you get older," "Children have no worries," or "Don't bother me with such trivial things," you have hurt your child's feelings and made him believe that his emotions are important to you. that you care about what it feels and that you are not indifferent to it.

Listen to your child! This command may seem trivial and obvious to you, but many parents hear but do not listen, ask but do not want to know. A simple consequence of not listening to a child's voice is that he or she runs away and locks himself in his own world. If a child is not listened to, he or she knows that there is no point in talking and that seeking your understanding and support will be of no use. They then gain the feeling that they are alone and have to deal with their problems and doubts alone, because they have no one to confide in and look in vain for reassurance, understanding, and kindness from their parents. As the years go by, isolation becomes more and more common. So if you didn't listen to your child with openness, curiosity, and passion, don't be surprised when a teenager or adult doesn't want to talk to you and has nothing to talk about because you once shut him up.

Exercise

Do you know your child?

› Do you know what your child dreams of?

› Do you know what he wants to be when he grows up?

› What are his passions, talents, and abilities, and in what direction they should be developed?

› Do you know what his favorite toy, food, or book is?

› Do you know what makes them sad and what makes them happy?

› Do you know where they would like to go on holiday? What movie should you go to the cinema to see?

› Do you know who he is friends with? How does he spend his free time? What does he do after school?

If you can answer all the questions without any doubt, you can consider that you know your child. However, if you hesitated even for a moment or answered "no" to any of the questions, it does not reflect well on you. Think about it, why don't you know this? Why isn't this important and engaging to you?

A child cannot communicate precisely and unambiguously, so it is extremely important to understand the child's world precisely to know the context of the statement. To understand the meaning, ask a series of supporting questions that will bring you as close as possible to the situation described by the child. Listen until the end, ask questions, and want to understand. When you listen carefully and show real interest, your child becomes convinced that he or she has an important place in your life, that he or she is valuable to you, and that you particularly care about him or her. Respond to him in an uplifting and constructive way. Remember that your view of reality is more mature, in-depth, and confirmed by experience, so rationally explain the world to your child instead of saying trivial phrases: "When you grow up, you will understand", and "These are not matters for children." Give him beautiful ideas about the world and its values, norms, and authorities. Don't scare yourself with the future by threatening: "Only life will teach you," "You'll see later." By saying this, you reinforce fear and shyness in the little person, make them helpless, take away their power and strength, and thus condemn them to be weak, helpless, and intimidated. Remember that the role of a parent is to give strength, fill with faith, make the child courageous and able to cope with difficulties, overcome obstacles, and recover from the disasters that will occur sooner or later. *It is from you that the child draws hope that it all makes sense and that life, despite hardships and disasters, is beautiful and should be lived as best as possible.* Enough bad things are happening around us, against our will, so don't spread bad visions about the future. Don't be a bad fortune teller for your child who predicts inevitable misfortune. That's not the role of a parent. Explaining reality, of course, does not involve coloring it or creating fairy-tale visions and illusions. **A child should know that there is evil, crime, injustice, and rudeness in the world and that there are brutal, false, and cynical people. Emphasize, however, that there are also heroes, people of action, brave and just, for whom sacrifice, honor, and goodness are words that have great meaning.**

Love your children!

For many years, your child has been fully dependent on you, both physically and emotionally. Like a sponge, it absorbs everything you give it and what you feed it, only to give it back to you in a few or a dozen years. If you give your child love and care, expect the same. And if you turn away from him and leave him to his own devices, be sure that he will do the same to you. Use this simple relationship and equip your child with positive emotions from the inside so that he or she becomes a good, happy, and fulfilled person. This isn't a particularly complicated task, you just need to be an emotionally intelligent parent.

Parental love is special and unique from other types of love because it is the only love that is unconditional. While parents or partners are loved for something (for what they give us or what they are like), a child is loved no matter what, without setting any conditions. Parental love is not subject to any "but" or "if...". Many parents emotionally manipulate their child, saying: "I will love you if...", using the feeling that the child needs so much to meet their own needs (e.g., to get back at their partner, they say: "Mommy will love you if... you won't go on vacation with daddy"). These types of messages are very harmful to a child's emotional development, they call into question the fact that he or she is worthy of love. He must be sure of your feelings regardless of what he does and what he will be like. Moreover, your child should have the belief that you will always help him no matter what, no matter what happens, and that you will not reject him. As long as you live and remain physically and mentally fit, parenthood obliges you to offer the best to your child.

Take notes!

Decide that for the next week you will tell your child at least twice a day (in the morning after waking up and in the evening before going to bed) that you love him and will always love him. Let your words be followed by actions - when you confess your love to your child, look into his eyes, hug him, and kiss him. Every day, observe your child's reactions to your declaration of love and write down your conclusions.

Conclusions: ....
....
....
....

Be persistent in showing your feelings, regardless of where you are in your life, what problems you are currently struggling with, and how your child behaves. Talk to your child and assure him of your love. It is not true that you can overdo it and that such a declaration will become boring or lose its value. Show affection: hug, kiss, stroke, touch. Physical contact gives children a sense of security and transmits good energy and warmth. Let your gestures and looks be filled with tenderness and full acceptance. A child must know that he or she is your most precious treasure, the greatest success in life.

Provide support, not criticism

Being a parent carries many responsibilities - one of them is the need to provide support. Support means that your child has unshakable confidence that they can always count on you and you will never let them down. He can always come to you with a problem and you will help him and stand by his side. Support is assurance that the future will be good because you are close and standing next to you. The parent's role is to shape the child's self-confidence and belief in his/her own value by recognizing his/her rights, showing him/her respect, and appreciating his/her achievements. Learn to notice and appreciate every effort your child makes, regardless of whether it brings the desired result. Promote attitudes of patience and perseverance in pursuing goals, expand possibilities, and give courage, encouragement, and hope in overcoming limitations. Give your child wings to fly to the sky, and don't trample them to the ground, burdening them with your problems, projecting your own fears, doubts, or excessive ambitions onto them.

There are a lot of parents who believe that children should be held short. Regardless of your opinion on praising children frequently, know that constant criticism and scolding lower the child's self-esteem so drastically that, despite possible successes, it will be difficult for him to believe in his own value and strength. Praise your child and brag about your child. Only lousy parents are dissatisfied with their children, complaining about them or berating them in front of others. They then prove to themselves that they should not have children and that they became parents by mistake. Give your child a kind and uplifting word. Remember that in the future it will face fierce competition, participate in a ruthless rat race, experience breakups, and struggle with problems. The words he will hear from you now may be the most important in his life - he will remember them during sleepless nights, and they will help him survive hard times and personal dramas. Give it to your child, don't let them go out into the world without your support. Keep telling him that he is smart, good, and beautiful, that he deserves all the best, and that he is worthy of the greatest love.

Ask yourself:
› What good things can I say about my child?
....
....

› Why do I think my child is wonderful and special?

....

....

› Why would I wish such a child for all parents?

....

....

› What qualities do I consider phenomenal in my child?

....

....

› Why am I proud of my child?

....

....

› When was the last time I told my child all of the above?

....

....

Parenting brings with it a sense of parental duty and commitment. The moment your baby comes into the world, you have a great responsibility that you cannot avoid. Parenting is about constant and reliable presence, safety, care, and support. The child should have the belief that he can rely on you and that you will not let him down. You are his first and most important role model, he imitates you and sets you as an example, trusting you implicitly. Try to cultivate this trust in such a way that the child feels that he can tell you about the worst thing he has done, and you will accept it with understanding and stand on his side. Even though you sometimes feel defenseless and weak, radiate strength and fortitude towards your child. When he is overwhelmed by the weight of worries, try to restore his peace and dispel his worries with kindness. When supporting your child, use subtle words and a gentle touch. Verbally and non-verbally tell him, "I understand you, I am with you."

Consistency, setting boundaries, predictability

An emotionally intelligent person is orderly, which means that what he does makes sense, is justified, and leads somewhere. Therefore, its activity has frames, delimitation points, and boundaries. This principle can be successfully applied to parenting. A good parent knows that you should not allow your child to do everything because it is not fulfilling his/her whims that make him/her wise and happy, but setting boundaries thanks to which he/she knows how to move in the world, what is good, what is bad, what path is worth taking, and which leads astray. Setting boundaries means clearly and unambiguously telling your child what behavior you tolerate and what behavior you discourage. Boundaries should be permanent, not fluid or conventional, regardless of the day or your mood. Parenting is about laying foundations.

Predictability is essential when creating boundaries. Parental behavior is predictable when the child knows what stimuli trigger specific reactions on your part (assuming, of course, that the reactions are adequate to the event; it is unacceptable for you to be offended at the child for accidentally breaking a vase, forbid him from meeting friends, etc.). The range of reactions a child sees should always be coherent, close to each other, and consistent. A serious parenting mistake is a situation when one day a child is severely punished for the same behavior, and on another day there is no reaction from the parent, and is even rewarded. This is a dysfunctional situation, because the child loses orientation in the scope of norms and values, and is engulfed in axio-normative chaos, which as a direct consequence may lead to pathological or deviant behavior.

Important rules

Regulations play an important role in various types of social organizations (military, police, enterprises). They are established so that the subordinate knows perfectly well what he can and should definitely not do, what actions are desirable and rewarded, and what is prohibited and severely punished. Suggest your child establish and sign the regulations. Prepare a large sheet of paper; it is best to hang the regulations on the wall in a visible place - so that you can always point your finger at its basic points and guidelines. Together with your child, determine which behaviors are affirmed and approved, and which ones are absolutely condemned (at the same time, explain to your child why certain excesses cannot be accepted, what their consequences are, and what the threats are). If the child complies with your arrangements (e.g. does not come home at the agreed time, gets into fights, does not do homework), remember to impose sanctions - appropriate to the offense.

Predictability applies not only to rewards and punishments but also - and perhaps above all - to how you treat the child and how you treat him or her. An intelligent parent should be characterized by emotional stability and balance. It is unacceptable for your child to be the object of your release - when you quarreled with your co-workers, your boss reprimanded you, your car broke down or your favorite sweater shrunk after washing. Some parents are so disturbed that they blame their children for their misfortunes, making them feel guilty and making them co-responsible for their failures.

Many children are deprived of their childhood and the carefreeness and freedom that comes with it. They must enter the adult world at a time when they should be children. Involving a child in conflicts between parents deprives him of inner joy, faith in people, optimism, and trust while causing a feeling of helplessness, meaninglessness, and apathy. In adulthood, such children must not only struggle with everyday problems but also carry the burden of childhood - they are unable to establish relationships, create lasting relationships, and attach to and trust another person. A red light and a warning keep flashing in their heads: "If my parents betrayed my trust, a stranger will do the same even more." The child is the victim of this tangled family puzzle. Meanwhile, it is the child who should be protected because he is completely defenseless, at the mercy of his parents or guardians, deprived of the choice of the situation he finds himself in and has to face.

Remember that the relationship with your child is not symmetrical - it does not involve an even division of tasks and responsibilities. You are the one who has to give without expecting anything in return. The asymmetrical relationship means that under no circumstances should you make your child the adult to take responsibility for your lack of responsibility. Don't mix up the roles - you are an adult and the child is a child who deserves safety, care, concern, and respect, and you have to provide it.

Fun fact

Parentification is the phenomenon of role reversal between parents and children. The child feels obliged to become an adult on an emotional level and take responsibility for the well-being of his parents. The effects of parentification are very harmful to the child's personality development. There is a gross violation of the boundaries separating the affairs of adults from those of children. The child stops demanding that his or her own needs be met, doing everything to meet the parents' needs. He tries to sense the parents' moods and tone down the conflict situation, divert attention, cover up arguments, and mediate. Psychologists dealing with structural family therapy (Salvador Minuchin, Braulio Montalvo, Bernice Rosman, Bernard Guerney, Florence Schumer) claim that parentification leads to serious disorders - the child in adulthood suffers from psychosomatic diseases, is unable to establish lasting bonds, is unable to take on a role parent, often becomes addicted and shows self-destructive tendencies. [Borchet, J., Lewandowska-Walter, A., & Rostowska, T., 2016; Van Loon, L. M. A., Van de Ven, M. O. M., Van Doesum, K. T. M., Hosman, C. M. H., & Witteman, C. L. M., 2017; van der Mijl, R. C. W., & Vingerhoets, A. J. J. M., 2017]

10 - INTELLIGENT EMOTIONAL BOSS

As you probably already know from reading the guide so far, emotional intelligence is a necessary skill in establishing and maintaining healthy interpersonal relationships, both in the personal and professional spheres. In the context of labor arrangements, hierarchy, status, and power, a high EI score becomes particularly important.

Power has always been attractive, especially to people who want to control the souls and minds of others. History shows that giving power to the wrong hands results in terror, violence, and human tragedies, which is why it should be exercised by emotionally healthy people. If an emotionally disturbed person takes power and his position becomes an instrument for treating his complexes, it will be dangerous. The pioneer of the sociology of emotions, Theodore Kemper, argues that power and status have a strong influence on emotions. This happens because power provides the ability to force others to follow the wishes and orders of those who wield it. Status, on the other hand, means receiving unforced respect and submission, recognition and prestige. Status and power determine the types of interactions – people like those who give them status; however, they do not like those who deprive them of their status or question it.[Turner, J. H., 2009; Turner, J.H., 2014]
An emotionally intelligent boss consciously uses both his own emotions and those of his team to expand and deepen his network

of interactions. Thanks to this, his crew is integrated, communicates clearly and directly, and in the event of a conflict, resolves it constructively and creatively. If you, as a boss, manage emotions effectively, you can influence the group so suggestively that individual and teamwork bring tangible benefits, even if individual team members differ from each other in terms of character or terms of style, or pace of work. Creating and maintaining healthy and symmetrical relationships in the team you supervise is as important as a high economic indicator and GDP growth. The work performed by subordinates is the result of their education and skills, but also how you treat these people, whether you understand and support them. A team led by an emotionally intelligent boss is more effective in its activities, more willing to take initiative, is open to new things and experiments, which allows it to achieve success and become a market leader.

Simply having power, prestige or a title is not enough to properly lead a group, engage and mobilize to action, or encourage discussion on introducing changes and improvements. Much more is needed - the ability to influence and shape collective emotions, to observe the emotional state of employees, what feelings promote their performance, and what feelings inhibit it. Make it a challenge to use emotional intelligence at work.

Exercise
Before you start reading in-depth about IE at work, answer the following two questions:
1. When will I know that employees are satisfied with their work and derive satisfaction from it?
....
....
2. When can you say that there is a good atmosphere at work?
....
....

Notice, appreciate, give thanks

For many people, work is a source of satisfaction and

fulfillment; a place where they pursue their chosen profession. This does not mean, of course, that there are no days when work is tiring, stressful, and exhausting. Sometimes the atmosphere becomes heavy and stuffy - conflicts break out, and misunderstandings occur, resulting in disagreements, plots, intrigues, and gossip. Then there is a tendency to complain or criticize the workplace or the boss and see him as the person responsible for the uncomfortable situation. This is a typical reaction and applies to almost the entire working population. Don't take it personally, and even allow employees to show their discontent and vent their grievances. This will effectively clear the atmosphere. You can relieve tension among employees in two ways:

1) behaviorally (organizing a weekend paintball trip, attaching punching bags to the ceiling, hanging a target in the company corridor at which employees can throw darts),

2) cognitively (proposing finding out the thoughts that cause them stress, reluctance, and bitterness, and thus depress them and discourage them from work).

The role of the boss is to create good relationships - those that contribute to effective work and cooperation. Good work is never the result of coercion or fear of the threat of dismissal but is a consequence of accepting co-responsibility for what is happening in the company and how the facility functions. For an employee to care about this, he or she must not perceive work as a necessary evil, a place where he or she only earns money and dreams of escaping from it as quickly as possible. If you want your team to consider work not only as a necessity but also as a value in itself, appreciate their efforts and show them the meaning of what they have achieved and what they have a chance to achieve. Recognize employees' ambitious ideas and create convenient opportunities to implement them.

Check it!

All the brilliant inventions that revolutionized the world were invented by accident. No one believed in their success or that they would become miracles of technology or art. Your employees' minds are also full of fantastic ideas - be willing to explore them and, if you can afford it, try to bring even the craziest project to life. Once a month, organize a brainstorming meeting - let employees come up with ideas on what could be improved at work and how to do it; let them say in what direction the company should develop, what branches should be strengthened, etc. Notice and reward the best ideas, even if the time for their implementation has not yet come.

The higher the boss's emotional intelligence score, the higher the work standards. From you, employees learn professionalism and respect for what they do. For them, you are an example of the organization of duties, professional ethos, and the ability to combine work and family life (remember flexible forms of employment and regulated working hours, even if you do not need such facilities yourself). If you like what you do and approach your activities with passion, reliability, and responsibility, and you also perform many tasks yourself, even though you can delegate them to others, you send a message to those around you: "Work is a value, I am proud of it, What am I doing". By presenting this attitude, you attract people who - by identifying with the "significant other" (see the box below) - copy your behavior and the way you approach responsibilities.

Keep it in mind!

For employees, the boss is a "significant other", which in sociological discourse means a person whose opinion we particularly care about, who is important to us, and towards whom we orient our behavior. Identification with a "significant other" is a social mechanism of identification with the values that this person professes and manifests in his way of being.

Develop the habit of recognizing and highlighting employee achievements (even small ones). Praise and thank them for their effort and commitment. Loudly express gratitude and even, in special situations, admiration. Introduce or maintain the all-American habit of patting yourself on the back and saying, "Good job!", as this is the best way to build your company's power. When employees feel appreciated and respected, they do their job willingly. Praise and words of appreciation have a positive effect - a satisfied employee works satisfactorily. Spread a positive aura around you, burst with good energy and enthusiasm - your attitude is key here. To see how much you can do and how much depends on you, imagine that you are conducting a large orchestra. Your task is to tune a multitude of different instruments into a perfect-sounding whole. Conduct in such a way that full tuning and euphony are possible - if you assign a task to be performed, take into account both the competencies and capabilities of the employees. If you know that average Joe feels best during speeches and lectures, and average John prefers to prepare reports, take their predispositions into account in the division of work. Never act against your will or force.

Excessive responsibilities, excessive ambitions, pressure and the need to meet market requirements cause burnout syndrome. Therefore, it is important to undertake projects that improve the physical and mental well-being of employees. You can do this by giving them memberships to a gym or a physical regeneration center, organizing integration trips or even coffee meetings. A large and unquestionable motivation is the social fund and the scope of gratuities. However, if you cannot afford bonuses or cash prizes, remember about symbolic awards.

Get to know the team inside out

As a boss, you determine the conditions and work system of your subordinates, influence the quality and pace of their actions, the level of commitment, perseverance and reliability in performing duties or assigned tasks. It's up to you what the atmosphere is like in the workplace, what relationships exist between employees, and what the degree of their professional bond is. Try to constantly examine the sociometric structure of the team, i.e. the distribution of mutual likes and dislikes. If you know who likes whom and who dislikes whom, it will be easier for you to select team members so that their mutual relations remain at least correct.

The creator of the sociometric structure is the Austrian-

American sociologist and psychiatrist Jacob Moreno. He noticed that in every team there are various types of dependencies resulting from the fact that you like a certain person, dislike someone, or are indifferent to someone. As a consequence, individual group members occupy various positions within it. So we can mention: a star (the most respected person, usually charismatic), cliques (subgroups within a group that close themselves off from the rest), and marginalized people (those who are pushed outside the mainstream of events). When you know a star in your team, you know who is trusted, and thus you can really influence the team and shape its work. It is worth turning the star into a person who supervises and is responsible for carrying out some tasks. Cliques should be broken up because they do not have a positive impact on the entire team and hinder the integration process. However, marginalized people can be tried to be included in the team's work, and if this fails, they should be considered as not meeting the company's profile. [Giacomucci, S., 2021]

Exercise

Ask employees to take a few minutes to complete a task to learn about the sociometry of the group. Ask them four questions about the people in their group. The answer to each question should be the name (and if the names are duplicated, then also the surname) of one person from the group.

› Who would you take to a desert island?
› Who wouldn't you hesitate to ask for help?
› Who couldn't you live in a hotel room with?
› Who wouldn't you treat to a second breakfast?

Knowing the answers to the above questions, you will know who is liked and who is not, whose company is desirable, and whose company is unwelcome.

Use this knowledge to divide activities, delegate certain tasks, share power, etc.

The condition for good work is reciprocity consisting of mutual assistance and exchange of information, knowledge, and experience. To develop this mutuality, the team must be integrated into a whole. An integrated team is one in which responsibility results from cooperation and co-decision - according to the principle of the four musketeers: "One for all, all for one." An emotionally intelligent boss should have a concept that unites the group he co-creates. People are different from each other, so a team integration model should take individual differences into account.

Guess who
Gather a group. Have each employee complete the sentences below and put their answers in the box. Then, one by one, pick out the cards, read their content aloud, and guess who wrote it. When naming a potential candidate, explain why you think so.
> IM good at...
> I do not like...
> I look like...
› What I most often do is...

Distance, superiority, emotional coldness, or misunderstood power

Many bosses, presidents, directors, managers and, broadly speaking, people in power suffer from insufficiently developed emotional intelligence. This deficit makes it very difficult for these people to recognize someone's effort and work, and to appreciate their commitment, abilities, and talents. They constantly criticize, condemn, and deprecate - most often because they know about their mediocrity and try hard to raise their self-esteem at the expense of others. By highlighting and pointing out other people's shortcomings and shortcomings, they put themselves in the position of an ideal person, free from faults and imperfections; the one who has a monopoly on knowledge. At the same time, by creating an intellectualized image of the Self, they turn on the mechanism of distracting attention from their own intellectual shallowness.

An emotionally intelligent person knows his limitations and realizes that, like Socrates, he really "knows nothing." With this awareness, he approaches others with openness and the attitude that he can learn a lot from them. He is steady and honest – there is consistency between what he says and does. If he does draw someone's attention, he uses substantive arguments that are supported by experience. If he lacks professional knowledge on a given topic, he remains silent.

High-quality work does not result from imposing an iron discipline on employees, keeping them at a distance, manifesting power and status in every possible context (referring to oneself as "president", introducing oneself, or signing with the name of the position or title). It is worth knowing that the social division between people who have power and those who are deprived of this power serves no purpose. Stratification prevents integration and community action. Try to maintain the principle of equality, remembering that each authority has a term of office and after some time someone else will take your place. Respect people, and treat them subjectively. Authoritarian and absolutist understanding of power and its exercise or creating distance causes reification (reification) instead of empathy. In turn, dehumanization breeds helplessness and passivity. So be cordial, friendly, and open to your employees. Of course, this is not about establishing intimate relationships, pretending closeness, or pretending friendship, but about understanding other people. If you don't take into account what he thinks and feels, you will never influence the way he works.

Examination
It's important that you know what your employees imagine is the right way to lead. So hand out the questionnaire interview form, which contains three questions:
› What does it mean to be a boss?
› What character traits should a good boss have?
› What would you expect from your boss in a problem situation?

By reading the answers carefully, you will find out what kind of boss your employees would like to have. Take this into account in your staff management and leadership process. Establish direct contact with your co-workers, build a relationship, and remember to constantly improve it. Try to personally get to know each person working in the company and remember their name and surname (which may be difficult in the case of teams of several hundred people). Set aside at least 20 minutes every day during which you will be at their disposal. Ask how they are feeling, if everything is OK, how their day is going. When you hear signs that someone is in trouble, do your best to help them.

Be professional!

Good power is power with good style. There is no place for dilettantes in personnel management, amateurism is excluded. Professionalism is about the ability to finalize matters and put into use good products, which is directly related to having expert knowledge and specialist proficiency in a given field. A professional does not disappoint, he guarantees certainty and quality of the service provided. Contracts with a specialist may be based on full trust. By working with such a person, you save time, money, and energy because you do not have to control his actions and resort to imposing sanctions in the event of failure to complete the task. From the point of view of social cooperation, this is beneficial because it minimizes the economic transaction costs associated with supervising and enforcing work. At work, a professional deal exclusively with work, separates private and professional matters, and does not combine interests. He does his job, i.e. what is the subject of the contract and for which he receives remuneration. At the emotional level, professionalism is visible in the skillful creation of relationships (uniting talented and passionate people around you, inspiring others with your attitude, mentoring) and organizing yourself emotionally.

Exercise
Are you a professional?
Only highlight the statements you believe to be true:
› If circumstances required working with someone I really disliked, I would take up the challenge.
› I can restrain myself even when I am very agitated.
› I always perform the tasks that fall within the scope of my responsibilities reliably.

› Mediocrity irritates me.
› I always keep my agreements.

Each underlined statement is worth one point. Five points mean complete professionalism; zero means that you are not a professional and you should work on the attributes necessary for a boss.

Bosses who have developed emotional intelligence can communicate - speak sensibly and listen carefully. They do not give orders, but consult; they do not get their own way, but strive for compromise; they do not require absolute obedience, but accept refusal and opposition. Above all, they sense individual and group emotions, and thus are able to create an atmosphere that allows them to work effectively and quickly. Remember that power obliges. Conduct yourself with class and elegance appropriate to the position in terms of style and manners. Be fair to employees and respect their dignity. Don't scold them, don't blackmail them with dismissal, don't take away bonuses for minor mistakes - treat them the way you would expect to be treated. If you have something to accuse them of, speak openly and clearly, call things by their name. Don't make malicious insults or innuendos - this only shows a lack of social skills and lowers your credibility. Be specific, factual, decisive and verbal, let your "yes" mean "yes" and your "no" mean "no". Keep your agreements, commitments and your word. A serious person does not mince words and does not promise anything that he cannot fulfill, that is beyond his capabilities. Messing around and pulling the wool over their eyes characterize buffoons and light-hearted people, but not people in positions of power who lead and direct others. So always take responsibility for your statements and actions. Be a model of reliability, accuracy and respect for the work performed.

BIBLIOGRAPHY

Ackerman, B. P., Abe, J. A., and Izard, C. E. (1998). Differential Emotions Theory and Emotional Development Mindful of Modularity. In Mascolo, M. F., and Griffin, S. (Eds.), What Develops in Emotional Development? New York: Plenum Press, pp 85–106.

Ackermann, H., Hage, S. R., and Ziegler, W. (2014). Brain mechanisms of acoustic communication in humans and nonhuman primates: An evolutionary perspective. Behavioral and Brain Sciences, 37(6), pp. 529–546.

Adelmann, P. K., and Zajonc, R. B. (1989). Facial efference and the experience of emotion. Annual Review of Psychology, 40, pp 249-280.

Bassett, D. S., & Gazzaniga, M. S. (2011). Understanding complexity in the human brain. Trends in cognitive sciences, 15(5), 200–209. https://doi.org/10.1016/j.tics.2011.03.006

Bernaras, E., Jaureguizar, J., & Garaigordobil, M. (2019). Child and Adolescent Depression: A Review of Theories, Evaluation Instruments, Prevention Programs, and Treatments. Frontiers in psychology, 10, 543. https://doi.org/10.3389/fpsyg.2019.00543

Beryce W. Maclennan (1961) Adolescent Aggression by Albert Bandura and Richard H. Walters, International Journal of Group Psychotherapy, 11:1, 94, DOI: 10.1080/00207284.1961.11508142

Bond, C. F., and DePaulo, B. M. (2006). Accuracy of deception judgments. Personality and Social Psychology Review, 10(3), pp 214-234.

Borchet, J., Lewandowska-Walter, A., & Rostowska, T. (2016). Parentification in late adolescence and selected features of the family system. Health Psychology Report, 4(2), 116–127. https://doi.org/10.5114/hpr.2016.55921

Brase, G.L. (2021). Leda Cosmides and John Tooby (Founders of Evolutionary Psychology). In: Shackelford, T.K., Weekes-Shackelford, V.A. (eds) Encyclopedia of Evolutionary Psychological Science. Springer, Cham. https://doi.org/10.1007/978-3-319-19650-3_3582

Bru-Luna LM, Martí-Vilar M, Merino-Soto C, Cervera-Santiago JL. Emotional Intelligence Measures: A Systematic Review. Healthcare (Basel). 2021 Dec 7;9(12):1696. doi: 10.3390/healthcare9121696. PMID: 34946422; PMCID: PMC8701889.

Burgoon, J. K. (2018). Micro expressions are not the best way to catch a liar. Frontiers in Psychology, 9.

Cacioppo, J. T., Hawley, L. C., & Bernston, G. G. (2003). The anatomy of loneliness. Current Directions in Psychological Science, 12(3), 71–74.

Carrere, S., Buehlman, K. T., Gottman, J. M., Coan, J. A., and Ruckstuhl, L. (2000). Predicting marital stability and divorce in newlywed couples. Journal of Family Psychology, 14(1), pp 42-58.

Chevalier-Skolnikoff, S. (1973). Facial expression of emotion in nonhuman primates. In Ekman, P. (Eds.), Darwin and Facial Expression. New York: Academic Press, pp 11-89. Chovil, N. (1991). Social determinants of facial displays. Journal of Nonverbal Behaviour, 15, Pp 141-154.

Christie, A., Jordan, P., Troth, A., & Lawrence, S. (2007). Testing the links between emotional intelligence and motivation. Journal of Management & Organization, 13(3), 212-226. doi:10.5172/jmo.2007.13.3.212

Coker, D. A., and Burgoon, J. K. (1987). The nature of conversational involvement and nonverbal encoding patterns. Human Communication Research, 13, pp 463-494.

Coyne, J. C., & Downey, G. (1991). Social factors and psychopathology: Stress, social support, and coping processes. Annual Review of Psychology, 42, 401–425.

Dattilio, F. M. (2000). Cognitive-behavioral strategies. In J. Carlson & L. Sperry (Eds.), Brief therapy with individuals &

couples (pp. 33–70). Zeig, Tucker & Theisen.

Dember, W. N., & Penwell, L. (1980). Happiness, depression, and the Pollyanna principle. Bulletin of the Psychonomic Society, 15(5), 321–323. https://doi.org/10.3758/BF03334546

Denault V., Plusquellec P., Jupe L. M., St-Yves M., Dunbar N. E., Hartwig M., Sporer S. L., Rioux-Turcotte J., Jarry J., Walsh D., Otgaar H., Viziteu A., Talwar V., Keatley D. A., Blandón-Gitlin I., Townson C., Deslauriers-Varin N., Lilienfeld S. O., Patterson M. L., . . . van Koppen P. J. (2020). The analysis of nonverbal communication: The dangers of pseudoscience in security and justice contexts. Anuario de Psicología Jurídica, 30(1), 1–12. Crossref

Dijk, C., Fischer, A. H., Morina, N., Van Eeuwijk, C., and Van Kleef, G. (2018). Effects of social anxiety on emotional mimicry and contagion: Feeling negative, but smiling politely. Journal of Nonverbal Behaviour, 42(1) pp 81-99.

Doob, A. N., & Wood, L. E. (1972). Catharsis and aggression: Effects of annoyance and retaliation on aggressive behavior. Journal of Personality and Social Psychology, 22(2), 156–162. https://doi.org/10.1037/h0032598

Eibl-Eibesfeldt, I. (1970). Ethology: The Biology of Behavior. San Francisco: Holt, Rinehart, and Winston.

Eibl-Eibesfeldt, I. (1971). Transcultural patterns of ritualized contact behavior. In Esser, A. H. (Eds.), Behavior and Environment. Boston, MA: Springer.

Eibl-Eibesfeldt, I. (1973). The expressive behaviour of the deaf-and-blind-born. In von Cranach, M., and Vine, I. (Eds.), Social Communication and Movement. European Monographs in Social Psychology, vol. 4. New York: Academic Press, pp 163-194.

Eibl-Eibesfeldt, I. (1989). Ethology: The Biology of Behavior. New York: Holt, Rinehart and Winston.

Eibl-Eibesfeldt, I. (2007). Human Ethology. London: Taylor and Francis.

Ekman, P. (1977). Facial Expression. Ch. 4. In Siegman, A., and Feldstein, S. (Eds.), Nonverbal Behavior and Communication. Mahwah, NJ: Lawrence Erlbaum Association, pp 97-116.

Ekman, P. (1993). Facial expression and emotion. American Psychologist, 48, PP 384-392. Ekman, P. (1994). Strong evidence for universals in facial expression: A reply to Russell's mistaken critique. Psychological Bulletin, 115, pp 268-287.

Ekman, P. (1998). Commentaries. In Darwin, C. (Eds.), The Expression of Emotion in Man and Animals, 3rd ed. New York: Oxford University press.

Ekman, P. (1999). Basic emotions. In Power, T. D. T. (Ed.), The Handbook of Cognition and Emotion. Sussex: Wiley, pp 45-60.

Ekman, P. (2001). Telling Lies: Clues to Deceit in the Marketplace, Politics, and Marriage. New

Ekman, P. (2003). Emotions Revealed: Recognizing Faces and Feelings to Improve Communication and Emotional Life. New York: Henry Holt.

Ekman, P., and Friesen, W. V. (1968). Nonverbal behavior in psychotherapy research. In Shlien, J. (Ed.), Research in Psychotherapy. Washington, DC: American Psychological Association, pp 179-216.

Ekman, P., and Friesen, W. V. (1969a). Nonverbal leakage and clues to deception. Psychiatry, 32(1), 88-106.

Ekman, P., and Friesen, W. V. (1969b). The repertoire of nonverbal behavior: Categories, origins, usage, and coding. Semiotica, 1, pp 49-98.

Ekman, P., and Friesen, W. V. (1971). Constants across cultures in the face and emotion. Journal of Personality and Social Psychology, 17, pp 124-129.

Ekman, P., and Friesen, W. V. (1972). Hand movements. Journal of Communication, 22, pp 353-374.

Ekman, P., and Friesen, W. V. (1975). Unmasking the Face: A Guide to Recognizing Emotions from Facial Clues. Englewood Cliffs, NJ: Prentice-Hall.

Ekman, P., and Friesen, W. V. (1976). Pictures of Facial Affect. Palo Alto, CA: Consulting Psychologists Press.

Ekman, P., and Friesen, W. V. (1978). Facial Action Coding System: A Technique for the Measurement of Facial Movement. Palo Alto, CA: Consulting Psychologists Press.

Ekman, P., Friesen, W. V., and Hager, J. C. (2002). Facial Action Coding System. Salt Lake City, UT: Research Nexus, Network Research Information.

Ekman, P., Friesen, W. V., and Tomkins, S. S. (1971). Facial affect scoring technique: A first validity study. Semiotica, 3, pp

37-58.

Ekman, P., Levenson, R. W., and Friesen, W. V. (1983). Autonomic nervous system activity distinguishes among emotions. Science, 22, pp 1208-1210.

Ekman, P., Sorenson, E. R., and Friesen, W. V. (1969). Pan-cultural elements in the facial display of emotions. Science, 164, pp 86-88.

Elam, K. K., Carlson, J. M., DiLalla, L. F., and Reinke, K. S. (2010). Emotional faces capture spatial attention in 5-year-old children. Evolutionary Psychology, 8(4), pp 754-767.

Elizabeth D. Hutchison, Dimensions of Human Behavior, Person and Environment · Volume 1, Sage Publications, 2008.

Floyd, K. (2006b). Communicating Affection: Interpersonal Behavior and Social Context. Cam- bridge: Cambridge University Press.

Frank, M. G., and Ekman, P. (1993). Not all smiles are created equal: The differences between enjoyment and non-enjoyment smiles. Humor, 6, pp 9-26.

Fredrickson BL. The role of positive emotions in positive psychology. The broaden-and-build theory of positive emotions. Am Psychol. 2001 Mar;56(3):218-26. doi: 10.1037//0003-066x.56.3.218. PMID: 11315248; PMCID: PMC3122271.

Fredrickson BL. What Good Are Positive Emotions? Rev Gen Psychol. 1998 Sep;2(3):300-319. doi: 10.1037/1089-2680.2.3.300. PMID: 21850154; PMCID: PMC3156001.

Galati, D., Sini, B., Schmidt, S., and Tnti, C. (2003). Spontaneous facial expressions in congenitally blind and sighted children aged 8-11. Journal of Visual Impairment and Blindness, 97, pp 418-428.

Giacomucci, S. (2021). Social work, sociometry, and psychodrama: Experiential approaches for group therapists, community leaders, and social workers. Springer Nature Singapore Pte Ltd.. https://doi.org/10.1007/978-981-33-6342-7

Goleman, D. (1996). Emotional Intelligence, Why It Can Matter More Than IQ. London: Bloomsbury.

Goodhart, D. E. (1985). Some psychological effects associated with positive and negative thinking about stressful event outcomes: Was Pollyanna right? Journal of Personality and Social Psychology, 48(1), 216–232. https://doi.org/10.1037/0022-

3514.48.1.216

Gunnery, S. D., and Hall, J. A. (2014). The Duchenne smile and persuasiveness. Journal of Nonverbal Behavior, 38, pp 181-194.

Hager, J. C., and Ekman, P. (1997). The asymmetry of facial actions is inconsistent with models of hemispheric specialization. In Ekman, P., and Rosenberg, E. (Eds.), What the Face Reveals. New York: Oxford University Press, pp 40-62.

Hart, S. D., Hare, R. D., & Harpur, T. J. (1992). The Psychopathy Checklist—Revised (PCL–R): An overview for researchers and clinicians. In J. C. Rosen & P. McReynolds (Eds.), Advances in psychological assessment, Vol. 8, pp. 103–130). Plenum Press. https://doi.org/10.1007/978-1-4757-9101-3_4

Hashim MJ. Patient-Centered Communication: Basic Skills. Am Fam Physician. 2017 Jan 1;95(1):29-34. PMID: 28075109.

Hess, U., Beaupre, M., and Cheung, N. (2002). To whom and why - cultural differences and similarities in the function of smiles. In Millicent, A. (Ed.), The Smile: Forms, Functions, and Consequences. New York: The Edwin Mellen Press, pp 187-216.

Izard CE. Emotion theory and research: highlights, unanswered questions, and emerging issues. Annu Rev Psychol. 2009;60:1-25. doi: 10.1146/annurev.psych.60.110707.163539. PMID: 18729725; PMCID: PMC2723854.

Izard, C. E. (1971). The Face of Emotion. New York: Appleton-Century-Crofts.

Izard, C. E. (1978). Emotions as motivations: An evolutionary-developmental perspective. In Dienstbier, R. A. (Ed.), Nebraska Symposium on Motivation, vol. 25. Lincoln: University of Nebraska Press, pp. 163–200.

Izard, C. E. (1994). Innate and universal facial expressions: Evidence from developmental and cross-cultural research. Psychological Bulletin, 115, pp. 288–299.

Izard, C. E., and Malatesta, C. (1987). Perspectives on emotional development: Differential emotions theory of early emotional development. In Osofsky, J. D. (Ed.), Handbook of Infant Development. New York: Wiley, pp 494–554.

Jessica L. Tracy , Joey T. Cheng , Richard W. Robins & Kali H. Trzesniewski (2009) Authentic and Hubristic Pride: The Affective Core of Self-esteem and Narcissism, Self and Identity, 8:2-3, 196-213, DOI: 10.1080/15298860802505053

Johnson, L. R., & LeDoux, J. E. (2010). Microcircuits of the amygdala. In G. M. Shepherd & S. Grillner (Eds.), Handbook of brain microcircuits (pp. 137–147). Oxford University Press. https://doi.org/10.1093/med/9780195389883.003.0014

Keltner, D. (1995). Signs of appeasement: Evidence for the distinct displays of embarrassment, amusement, and shame. Journal of Personality and Social Psychology, 68(3), pp 441-454.

Koole, S. L., Veenstra, L., Domachowska, I., Dillon, K. P., & Schneider, I. K. (2022). Embodied anger management: Approach-oriented postures moderate whether trait anger becomes translated into state anger and aggression. Motivation Science, 8(2), 174–190. https://doi.org/10.1037/mot0000257

LeDoux J. (2012). Rethinking the emotional brain. Neuron, 73(4), 653–676. https://doi.org/10.1016/j.neuron.2012.02.004

LeDoux, J. E. (1992). Emotion and the amygdala. In J. P. Aggleton (Ed.), The amygdala: Neurobiological aspects of emotion, memory, and mental dysfunction (pp. 339–351). Wiley-Liss.

Luck, T., Luck-Sikorski, C. The wide variety of reasons for feeling guilty in adults: findings from a large cross-sectional web-based survey. BMC Psychol 10, 198 (2022). https://doi.org/10.1186/s40359-022-00908-3

Magnano, Paola, Craparo, Giuseppe, & Paolillo, Anna. (2016). Resilience and Emotional Intelligence: which role in achievement motivation. International Journal of Psychological Research, 9(1), 9-20. Retrieved November 06, 2023, from http://www.scielo.org.co/scielo.php?script=sci_arttext&pid=S2011 -20842016000100002&lng=en&tlng=en.

Marazziti, D., Veltri, A., & Piccinni, A. (2018). The mind of suicide terrorists. CNS Spectrums, 23(2), 145-150. doi:10.1017/S1092852917000566

Matsumoto, C. (1987). Dance research: Problem situation and learning of problem solving II: Qualities of movements and feeling values. Bulletin of Japan Association of Physical Education for Women, 87(1), pp 53-89.

Matsumoto, D. (1991). Cultural influences on facial expressions of emotion. Southern Communication Journal, 56, pp 128-137.

Matsumoto, D. (2006). Culture and nonverbal behaviour. In Manusov, V., and Patterson, M. L. (Eds.), The Sage Handbook of

Nonverbal Communication. London: Sage, pp 219-235.
Matsumoto, D., and Hwang, H. S. (2011). Evidence for training the ability to read micro-expressions of emotion. Motivation and Emotion, 35, pp 181-191.

Matsumoto, D., and Hwang, H. C. (2017). Methodological issues regarding cross-cultural studies of judgments of facial expressions. Emotion Review, 9(4), pp 375-382.

Matsumoto, D., LeRoux, J., Wilson-Cohn, C., Raroque, J., Kooken, K., Ekman, P., Yrizarry, N., Loewinger, S., Uchida, H., Yee, A., Amo, L., and Goh, A. (2000). A new test to measure emotion recognition ability: Matsumoto and Ekman's Japanese and Caucasian brief affect recognition test (JACBART). Journal of Nonverbal Behavior, 24, pp 179-209.

Matsumoto, D., Takeuchi, S., Andayani, S., Kouznetsova, N., and Krupp, D. (1998). The contribution of individualism-collectivism to cross-national differences in display rules. Asian Journal of Social Psychology, 1, pp 147-165.

Matsumoto, D., Yoo, S. H., Hirayama, S., and Petrova, G. (2005). Development and validation of a measure of display rule knowledge: The display rule assessment inventory. Emotion, 5(1), pp 23-40.

Mayer, J. D., Caruso, D. R., & Salovey, P. (1999). Emotional intelligence meets traditional standards for an intelligence. Intelligence, 27 (4), 267-298.

McAdams, D. P., Jackson, R. J., and Kirshnit, C. (1984). Looking, laughing, and smiling in dyads as a function of intimacy motivation and reciprocity. Journal of Personality, 52, PP 261-273.

Muniruzzaman, M. Transformation of intimacy and its impact in developing countries. Life Sci Soc Policy 13, 10 (2017). https://doi.org/10.1186/s40504-017-0056-8

Muris, P., Merckelbach, H., Otgaar, H., & Meijer, E. (2017). The malevolent side of human nature: A meta-analysis and critical review of the literature on the dark triad (narcissism, Machiavellianism, and psychopathy). Perspectives on psychological science, 12(2), 183-204.

O'Connor PJ, Hill A, Kaya M, Martin B. The Measurement of Emotional Intelligence: A Critical Review of the Literature and Recommendations for Researchers and Practitioners. Front Psychol. 2019 May 28;10:1116. doi: 10.3389/fpsyg.2019.01116.

PMID: 31191383; PMCID: PMC6546921.

Plutchik R., Emotion: A psychoevolutionary synthesis, Harper & Row, Nowy Jork 1980, s. 10–15.

Salovey, P., & Mayer, J. D. (1990). Emotional Intelligence. Imagination, Cognition and Personality, 9(3), 185-211. https://doi.org/10.2190/DUGG-P24E-52WK-6CDG

Schneider, K., and Josephs, I. (1991). The expressive and communicative functions of preschool children's smiles in an achievement situation. Journal of Nonverbal Behavior, 15, pp 185-198.

Sluckin, W. (Ed.). (1979). Fear in Animals and Man. New York: Van Nostrand Reinhold. Smith, J., Chase, J., and Lieblich, A. (1974). Tongue showing. Semiotica, 11(3), pp 201-246.

Soderkvist, S., Ohlen, K., and Dimberg, U. (2018). How the experience of emotion is modulated by facial feedback. Journal of Nonverbal Behaviour, 42, pp 129-151.

Stephen K. Rice, (2009), Emotions and terrorism research: A case for a social-psychological agenda, Journal of Criminal Justice, Volume 37, Issue 3, Pages 248-255, ISSN 0047-2352, https://doi.org/10.1016/j.jcrimjus.2009.04.012.

Stern, D. N. (2007). Applying developmental and neuroscience findings on other-centered participation to the process of change in psychotherapy. In Braten, S. (Ed.), On Being Moved: From Mirror Neurons to Empathy, Amsterdam: John Benjamins, pp 35-47.

Takahashi, A., & Miczek, K. A. (2014). Neurogenetics of aggressive behavior: studies in rodents. Current topics in behavioral neurosciences, 17, 3–44. https://doi.org/10.1007/7854_2013_263

Tracy, J. C., and Matsumoto, D. (2008). The spontaneous expression of pride and shame: Evidence for biologically innate nonverbal displays. Proceedings of the National Academy of Sciences, 105, pp 11655-11660.

Turner, J. H. (2009). The Sociology of Emotions: Basic Theoretical Arguments. Emotion Review, 1(4), 340-354. https://doi.org/10.1177/1754073909338305

Turner, J.H. (2014). Emotions, Sociology of. In The Wiley Blackwell Encyclopedia of Health, Illness, Behavior, and Society (eds W.C. Cockerham, R. Dingwall and S. Quah). https://doi.org/10.1002/9781118410868.wbehibs504

Twardosz, S., Botkin, D., Cunningham, J. K., Weddle, K., Sollie, D., and Schreve, C. (1987). Expression of affection in daycare. Child Study Journal, 17, 133-151.

van der Mijl, R. C. W., & Vingerhoets, A. J. J. M. (2017). The positive effects of parentification: An exploratory study among students. Psihologijske Teme, 26(2), 417–430.

Van Loon, L. M. A., Van de Ven, M. O. M., Van Doesum, K. T. M., Hosman, C. M. H., & Witteman, C. L. M. (2017). Parentification, stress, and problem behavior of adolescents who have a parent with mental health problems. Family Process, 56(1), 141–153. https://doi.org/10.1111/famp.12165

Voss RM, M Das J. Mental Status Examination. [Updated 2022 Sep 12]. In: StatPearls [Internet]. Treasure Island (FL): StatPearls Publishing; 2023 Jan-. Available from: https://www.ncbi.nlm.nih.gov/books/NBK546682/

Watson, N. M., Wells, T. J., and Cox, C. (1998). Rocking chair for dementia patients: Its effect on psychosocial well-being and balance. American Journal of Alzheimer Disease and Other Dementias (November), pp. 296-308.

Winter J., Currier C. (2015). TSA's secret behavior checklist to spot terrorists. The Intercept. https://theintercept.com/2015/03/27/revealed-tsas-closely-held-behavior-checklist-spot-terrorists/

Worcel, S. D., Shields, S., and Paterson, C. A. (1999). "She looked at me crazy": Escalation of conflict through telegraphed emotions. Adolescence, 34, p 689.

Wurman, R. S. (1989). Information Anxiety: What to Do When the Information Doesn't Tell You What You Need to Know. New York: Bantam Books.

York: W. W. Norton and Co.

Zajonc, R. B. (1965). Social facilitation. Science, 149, pp 269–274.

Zajonc, R. B. (1980). Compresence. In Paulus, P. B. (Ed.), Psychology of Group Influence. Hillsdale, NJ: Lawrence Erlbaum Associates, pp 35-60.

Zajonc, R. B. (2001). Mere exposure: A gateway to the subliminal. Current Directions in Psychological Science, 10(6), pp 224-228.

Zajonc, R. B., Murphy, S. T., and Inglehart, M. (1989). Feeling and facial efference: Implications of the vascular theory of emotion. Psychological Review, 96(3), pp 395-416.

Zandonella, C. (2016). Electron-photon small-talk could have big impact on quantum computing. Princeton University News. princeton.edu (accessed September 27, 2020).

Zheng, X., Wu, B., Li, C. S., Zhang, P., & Tang, N. (2021). Reversing the Pollyanna effect: The curvilinear relationship between core self-evaluation and perceived social acceptance. Journal of Business and Psychology, 36(1), 103–115. https://doi.org/10.1007/s10869-019-09666-3